CROSSED™

Wish You Were Here

VOLUME 4

SIMON SPURRIER story

FERNANDO MELEK artwork

JUANMAR color

JACEN BURROWS covers

JAYMES REED letters

WILLIAM CHRISTENSEN editor-in-chief
MARK SEIFERT creative director
JIM KUHORIC managing editor
DAVID MARKS director of events
ARIANA OSBORNE production assistant

CROSSED CREATED BY GARTH ENNIS

www.crossedcomic.com www.avatarpress.com www.twitter.com/avatarpress

CROSSED Wish You Were Here Volume 4. August 2014. Published by Avatar Press, Inc., 515 N. Century Blvd. Rantoul, IL 61866.

SIMON SPURRIER FERNANDO MELEK

CROSSED

VOLUME FOUR

Wish You Were Here

CRITICAL MASS.
ENTRY #46. YEAH. LET'S TALK ABOUT CRITICAL MASS.
FOR ALL THE PRACTICED NUMBNESS, ALL THE UNFLAPPABILITY AND THOU-SHALT-NOT-DAYDREAM APATHY...
...SOONER OR LATER, DIARY?
STRAW.
CAMEL'S BACK.
SNAP.
CRITICAL MASS.
TERMINAL VELOCITY.
SHEER IDIOT COWARDICE.
CHOOSE YOUR PREFERRED TERM.

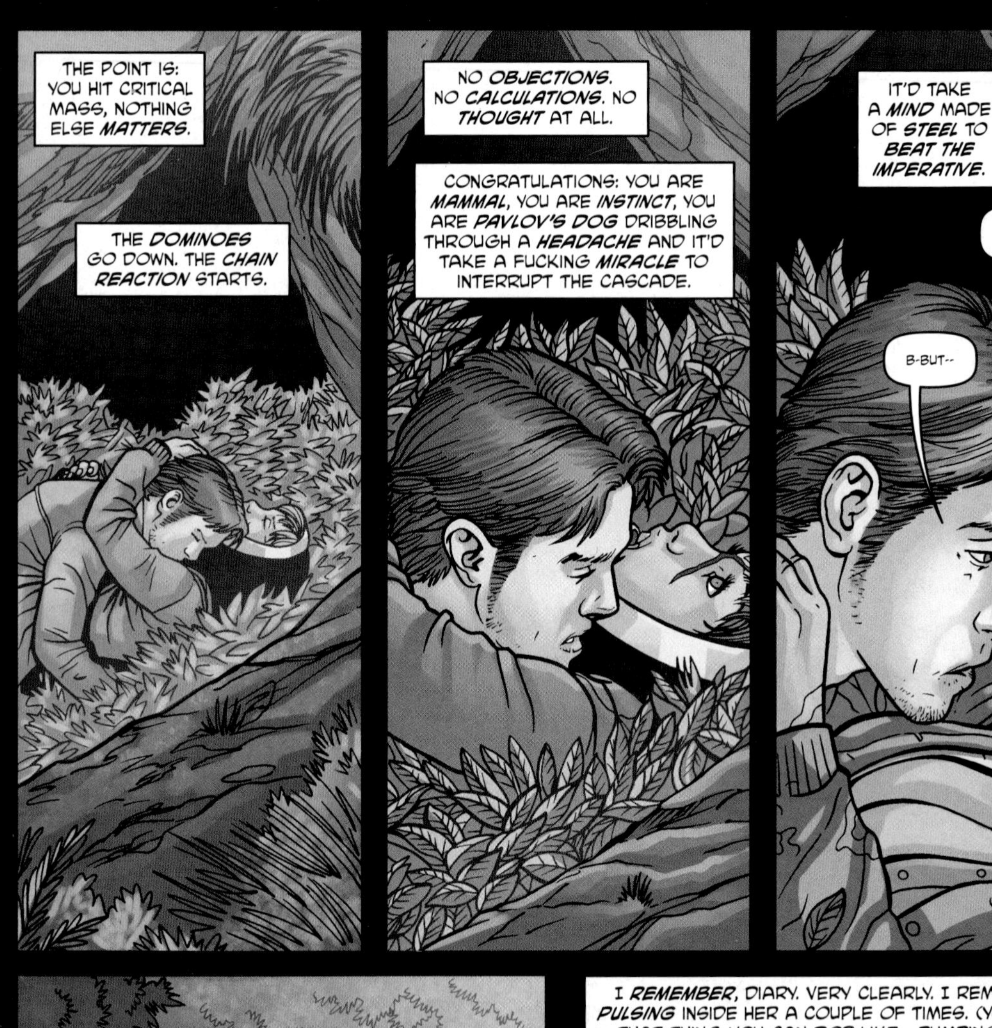
THE POINT IS: YOU HIT CRITICAL MASS, NOTHING ELSE MATTERS.
THE DOMINOES GO DOWN. THE CHAIN REACTION STARTS.
NO OBJECTIONS. NO CALCULATIONS. NO THOUGHT AT ALL.
CONGRATULATIONS: YOU ARE MAMMAL, YOU ARE INSTINCT, YOU ARE PAVLOV'S DOG DRIBBLING THROUGH A HEADACHE AND IT'D TAKE A FUCKING MIRACLE TO INTERRUPT THE CASCADE.
IT'D TAKE A MIND MADE OF STEEL TO BEAT THE IMPERATIVE.
STOP.
B-BUT--
STOP.

I REMEMBER, DIARY. VERY CLEARLY. I REMEMBER PULSING INSIDE HER A COUPLE OF TIMES. (YOU KNOW THAT THING YOU CAN DO? LIKE... PUMPING YOUR PROSTATE OR WHATEVER IT IS. A DEEP-DOWN TWITCH.)

COULDN'T STOP MYSELF. COULDN'T... COULDN'T BEAR THAT HER ATTENTION WASN'T ON ME.

EVEN IN THE FACE OF HORROR: DOMINOES.

STOP IT.

NOON, LYNESS BEACH. AS PLANNED-- AND THAT'S THE LAST TIME YOU'LL READ THOSE WORDS IN THIS DIARY FOR A LONG FUCKING WHILE.
WHAT 'APPENED?
WHERE'S JACKSON, MATE?

AH BUGGER.

OKAY. I SHOULD COME CLEAN. IT'S BEEN SEVERAL DAYS SINCE ALL THIS HAPPENED. BUSY FUCKING DAYS. AWFUL FUCKING DAYS.
A LOT'S GONE ON.
A LOT'S GONE ON AND NOW THERE'S TIME TO REFLECT AND YOU WANT TO KNOW THE OTHER THING, DIARY, THAT ALWAYS DEFINES CRITICAL MASS?

IT CAN'T SUSTAIN. IT EITHER *ERUPTS* OR *DISSOLVES.*

BUT ONE WAY OR THE *OTHER?* THERE'S *ALWAYS* AN AFTERMATH.

CALL IT THE FUCKING COULDAWOULDASHOULDA STAGE.

(COULDA CONFRONTED HIM. WOULDA ASKED QUESTIONS IF I'D THOUGHT OF IT.)
(SHOULDA SHOT HIM. IN THE FACE. OVER AND OVER. FOREVER.)

BUT THINGS NEVER GO THE HOLLYWOOD WAY. WE KNOW THAT.
AND WHETHER YOUR CRITICAL MASS EXPLODES OR FIZZLES OUT--
WE'VE. WE'VE GOT TO GET OUT OF H--
BUT HE'S GONE.
--IT'S NEVER THE OPTION YOU WANT.
GET OFF. GET...
OUT
GET OUT OF M.
HH.
STEEL. SLAMMING DOWN. SHUTTING IT OUT.
RESISTING THE WORLD.
WE'RE LEAVING. NOW.
BUT I DIDN'T EVEN C
NOW.
THIS WORLD. THIS WORLD.
THE CHAIN REACTIONS YOU WANT? NUH-UH.
NEVER THE WAY YOU'D LIKE. DISSOLVE, SPUTTER-OUT, FADE AWAY.
ANTI. FUCKING. CLIMAX.
--S THIS DAY OUR DAILY BREAD AND FORGIVE US OUR T...
...OUR TRESPASSES, A-AS WE FORGIVE THOSE WHO'VE--

AND THE CHAIN REACTIONS YOU DON'T WANT? EVEN WHEN YOU'RE... YOU'RE SLUMPED EXHAUSTED IN THE AFTERMATH OF A RECENTLY-CONCLUDED FUCKING HORROFEST?
H-HEY.
YOU HEAR BELLS--?
G.
GUYS?
EVEN WHEN YOU'VE SURVIVED, DIARY, AND THE CAPACITY TO THINK'S FINALLY COMING BACK AND YOU THINK, HAHAHA, YOU THINK LIFE IS A WAVEFORM, AND AFTER THE RUSH THERE'S GOT TO BE A QUIET SPELL...
...EVEN THEN, EVEN THEN--

THE DOMINOES.
WHAT'S

KEEP ON.

FALLING.
NO.

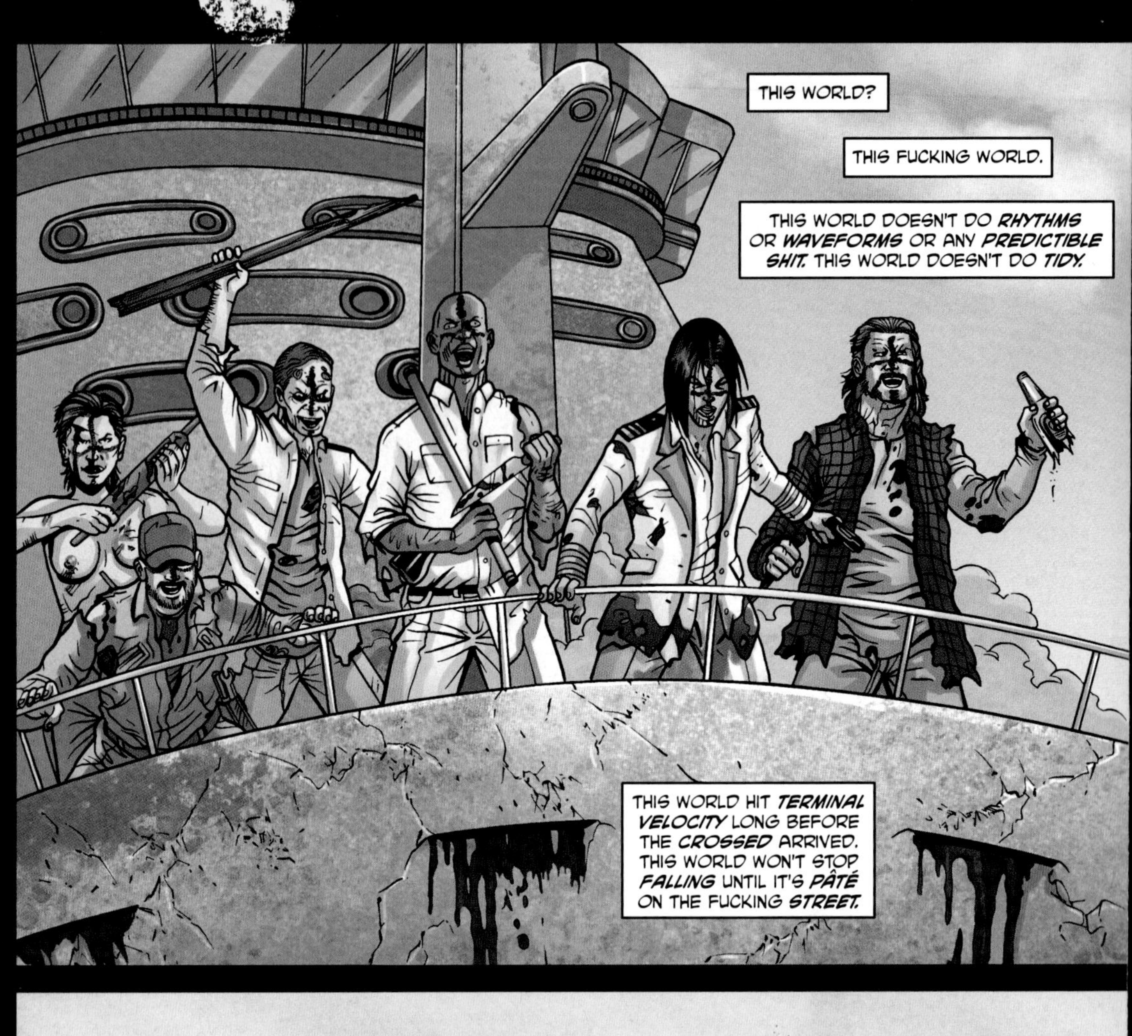
THIS WORLD?
THIS FUCKING WORLD.
THIS WORLD DOESN'T DO *RHYTHMS* OR *WAVEFORMS* OR ANY *PREDICTIBLE SHIT.* THIS WORLD DOESN'T DO *TIDY.*
THIS WORLD HIT *TERMINAL VELOCITY* LONG BEFORE THE *CROSSED* ARRIVED. THIS WORLD WON'T STOP *FALLING* UNTIL IT'S *PÂTÉ* ON THE FUCKING *STREET.*

THIS WORLD *IS* CRITICAL MASS.

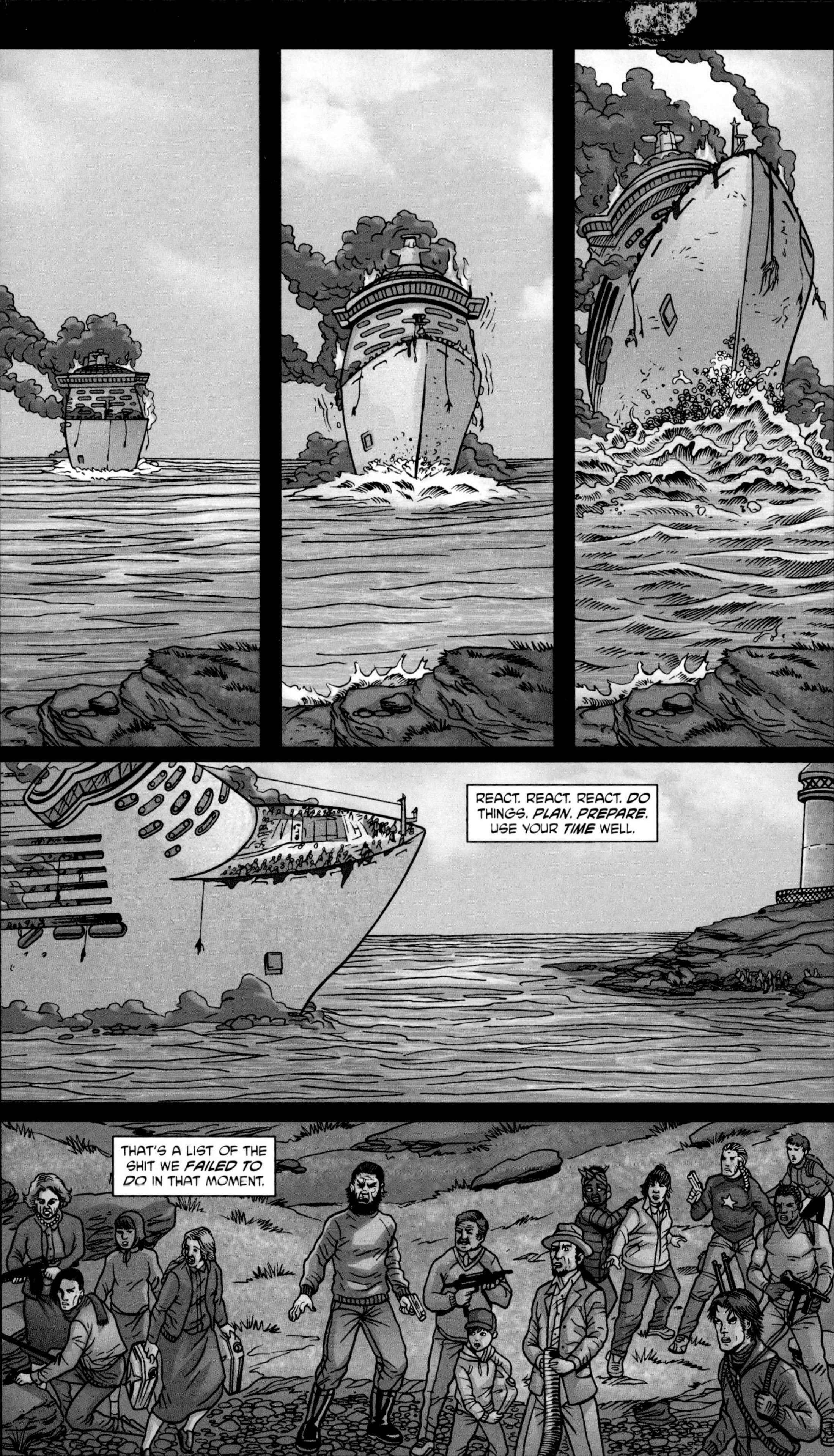
REACT. REACT. REACT. *DO* THINGS. *PLAN. PREPARE.* USE YOUR *TIME* WELL.
THAT'S A LIST OF THE SHIT WE *FAILED TO DO* IN THAT MOMENT.

HA!
HA HA HARAAAAAAAAAAAAAA
LUCKY FOR US PLANNING'S NOT THEIR STRONGPOINT, EITHER.
JUST REACTION.
REACTION AND CUNNING.
AND HATE.
AND JOY.
BURN.

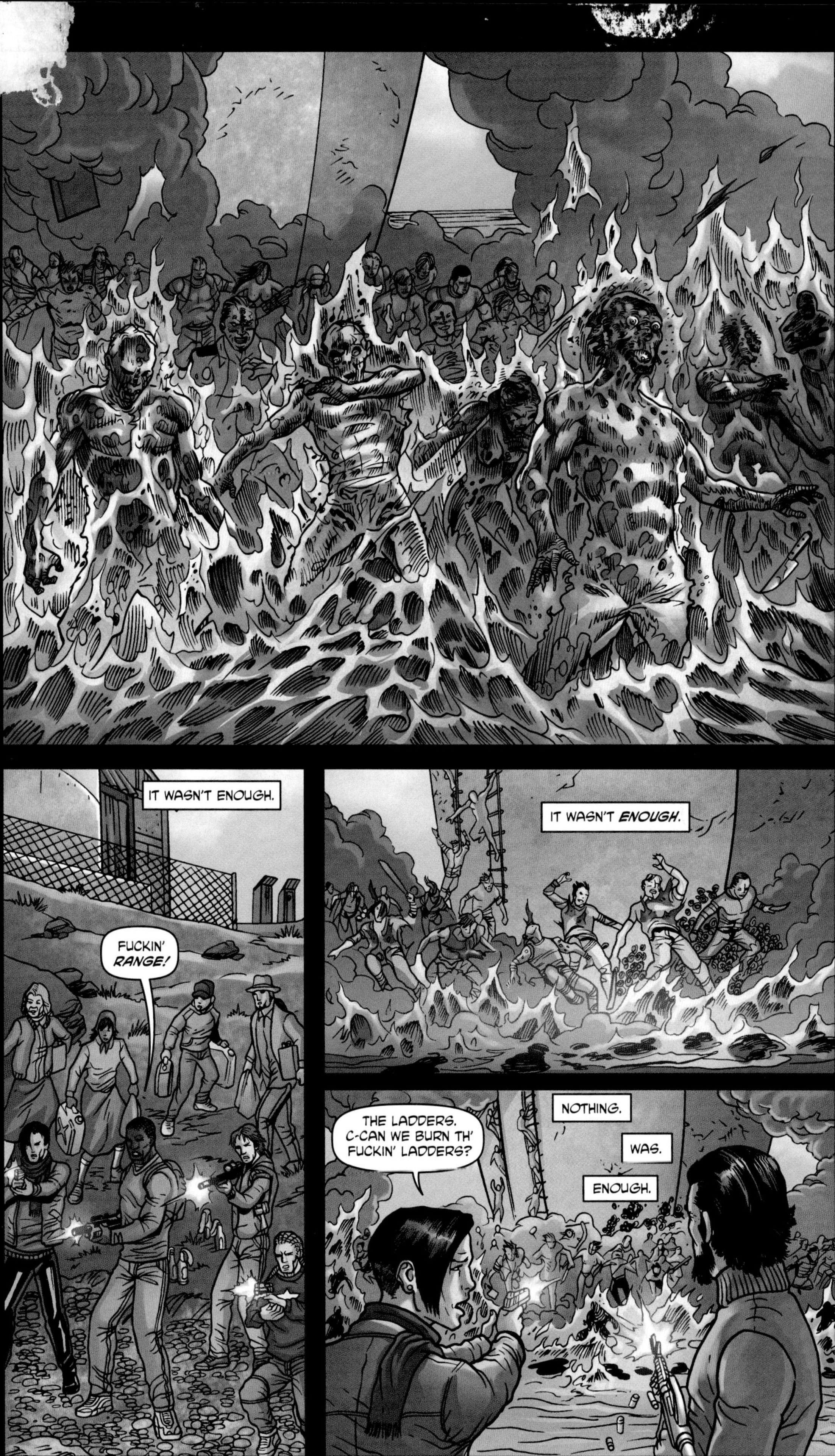
IT WASN'T ENOUGH.
FUCKIN' RANGE!
IT WASN'T ENOUGH.
THE LADDERS. C-CAN WE BURN TH' FUCKIN' LADDERS?
NOTHING.
WAS.
ENOUGH.

YES WE CAN.
HEH.
OH.
GEDDOWN, PET!
DOWN!
CHRISTINE?

I THINK I SAW CAPTAIN DORA GO DOWN. HAIR ALIGHT. FACE TWISTED.
HARD TO SAY. MORE KEPT POURING-IN.
OTHERS COMING ROUND THE FUCKING SIDES. CHAOS. BELLS RINGING, LANGALANGLANGALANG.
ONLY REALLY A MATTER OF TIME BEFORE SOMEONE-- THE LEADER, IN FACT; THE INSTINCTIVE FUCKING LEADER TO WHOM ALL MUST TURN IN MOMENTS OF HORROR--
--BEFORE THAT LEADER SAID:
PULL BACK.
YOU WOT?
WE. WE HAVE TO.
WE... WE USE THE DEFENCES. OTHER SIDE. LET THEM TRY TO COME THROUGH. WHITTLE THEM DOWN.
BUT... BUT THAT'S THE WRONG DIRECTION! EDEN'S SPOSEDA TO BE THE BLOODY SAFE SIDE!
EDEN'S ALREADY FUCKED. WE DON'T KNOW HOW MANY SLIPPED INLAND, WHAT WEAPONS THEY'VE GOT. OTHER SIDE'S THE ONLY PLACE WE KNOW THEY'RE NOT.
HE'S RIGHT.
PULL BACK!
'ANG ABOUT-- WHERE THE FUCK'RE YOU GOING?

I.
THERE'S JUST SOMETHING I NEED TO... I'LL... I'LL JUST BE A *SECOND*.
FUCKING *WAIT* FOR ME!
A *PEN*.
OF ALL THE THINGS. A PEN TO REPLACE THE ONE I LOST.
SUDDENLY SO FUCKING *IMPORTANT*. IN THE FACE OF CARNAGE. IN THE FACE OF LOSS, MY BRAIN SNUCK OFF TO YOU, IT NEEDED *YOU*, AND I'M WRITING IN YOU *NOW* SO YOU KNOW I *GOT* ONE BUT.
BUT. STILL. IT'S STUPID.
A LIFE SO EMPTY, IT'LL RISK ITSELF FOR A BOOK NOBODY WILL READ.
ULTIMATE *NARCISSISM* OR ULTIMATELY *PATHETIC?*

DIDN'T KNOW WHAT TO DO, DIARY. BROKEN. SPINELESS. *WORDLESS*.

TURNS OUT *STUPIDITY* CAN HIT *CRITICAL MASS* TOO.

IN THE END THE FUCKING *HOLLYWOOD BULLSHIT* THAT SPRUNG TO MIND WAS:

BABY.
UH?
M-MIDDLE OF THE *ROAD.*
ACTUAL HUMAN BABY.
YOU'RE... NAH. YOU'RE *IMAGINING* TH
FUCK ME.

YYYYYYOU
SSSHHHHH
F-FUCK!
N
Y
YOU
BUT.
WH.

PEN.
PEN.
PEN
PEN
PEN

AMINAH!
AMINAAAAAAAAHHH!
RANGE.
IT TOOK A WHILE, I SUPPOSE. I DON'T REALLY *REMEMBER*.
THE DEFENCES DID THEIR *BIT*. RAZORWIRE. SPIKES.
BULLETS BULLETS BULLETS BULLETS.
THEY ALL DID THEIR *BIT*.
WE "WON".
SHITE.

AND THEN WE DIDN'T.
CRITICAL MASS.
DECISIONS THAT CAN'T BE HELD-OFF. HANDS GET FORCED, BRAINS GET BUMPED. IMPERATIVES MASQUERADING AS CHOICES.
YOU COME DOWN TO IT, TIMES LIKE THOSE, AND REALLY? THE ONLY CHOICE IS WHO SAYS IT FIRST.
THE LEADER OR THE CHIEFTAIN?
GET TH' BOATS.
EH?
WE.
WE HAVE T'GET THE FUCK OFFA THIS ISLAND.

DIARY: WE LEFT.
DO YOU UNDERSTAND? DO YOU UNDERSTAND WHAT THAT MEANS?
WE LEFT AND NONE OF IT FELT REAL AND IN ALL THE RUSH, IN ALL THE RUSH I DIDN'T GET A CHANCE TO THINK ABOUT IT.
THE ISLAND. MY ISLAND.

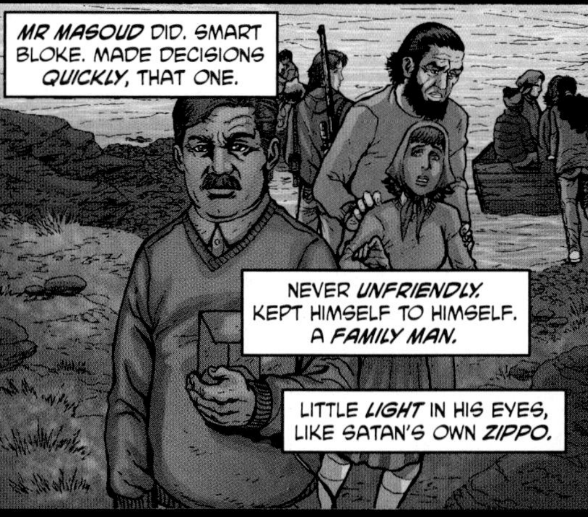
MR MASOUD DID. SMART BLOKE. MADE DECISIONS QUICKLY, THAT ONE.
NEVER UNFRIENDLY. KEPT HIMSELF TO HIMSELF. A FAMILY MAN.
LITTLE LIGHT IN HIS EYES, LIKE SATAN'S OWN ZIPPO.

LOST HIS SON LAST AUTUMN. HADN'T BEEN RIGHT SINCE.
LOST HIS WIFE MINUTES BEFORE.
CRITICAL MASS. CRITICAL MASS. IMPERATIVES MASQUERADING AS CHOICES.

MAKE THE DECISION-- LIKE YOU'VE GOT A CHOICE--
--AND NEVER MIND WHAT'S LEFT BEHIND.
DAAAADDDEEEEEEE--

BUT THAT'S THIS WORLD ALL OVER, ISN'T IT?
NEVER MIND WHAT'S LEFT BEHIND.

DIARY, WE HAD TWO CLAYMORES LEFT FROM THE SORTIE.

NOW WE HAVE ONE.

THE KID *PASSED OUT.* I REMEMBER THINKING: THANK *CHRIST.*
NOW I CAN GET BACK TO *WALLOWING* IN *MY OWN* SHIT.

CHANCE TO THINK IT THROUGH, AT LAST. YOU KNOW WHAT IT FELT LIKE?

FELT LIKE *PANIC.* FLOATING AWAY FROM *HOME,* WATCHING THEM *DANCE* ON *OUR* SHORE. *FIRES* CREEPING. *SHEEP* SCREAMING. COUPLE OF PLUSSIES RUSHING AFTER US INTO THE WATER. DIDN'T GET FAR.

WE SHOULDN'T HAVE LEFT.

TOOK ME THAT LONG TO REALISE IT.

MY *ISLAND.*
AFTER EVERYTHING. EVERYTHING I'VE *DONE* FOR IT.

L-LOOK, AFTER EVERYTHING WE WENT THROUGH WITH ASHOKE... THE LAST THING WE NEED IS ANOTHER LIABI--
DAWAY!
UP! UP!
HHH.
A-AT LEAST TRY TO KEEP IT QUIET.
"HER."
AEOLIEANN THIS... THIS IS SUCH A BAD IDEA I CAN'T EVEN BEGIN TO--
I COULDN'T LEAVE A CHILD, SHAKY. AN' YOU WOULDN'T ASK ME TO.
F-FINE, I KNOW, BUT...
WE NEED TO STOP AND THINK AB--
SHH.
CAN... CAN YOU H...
CAN YOU HEAR PRAYING?

EDITH GOT-ON WITH THE GODBOTHERING AS WE ROWED. MARIA TOO. EVEN *SELINE* JOINED IN WHEN HER BRAIN WASN'T *SPINNING*.
A FUCKING HAND-HOLDING *CIRCLEJERK* TO MARK THE EXODUS-- *"THE LAND OF NOD,"* ONE MUMBLED, *"EAST OF EDEN"* --WHILE ROSHAN CRIED IN HER SLEEP AND MIRANDA WONDERED WHERE MARK WENT AND...
AND SKIP SAID:
OH.
FFFFFFFUCK
DOMINOES.
THEY SLUNK OUT, DIARY, LIKE A *WHISPER*.
LIKE... HA.

LIKE A *PRAYER*.

ALL THE *X*-FACES. THE ONES SHE *MARKED*. ALL THE *GUNS* FROM THE DRIFTFLEET.

ARE THEY A... WHAT? AN *INNER CIRCLE*? IS *THAT IT?* LIKE, THE ONES SHE CAN *TRUST?* THE ONES LIKE *JACKSON* SAID-- LIKE *SELINE* SAID.

NOT RUSHING IN. *NOT* GOING FOR THE KILL. *SAVOURING*. ENJOYING THE *BUILDUP*.

THE ONES SHE'S TAUGHT A LITTLE FUCKING *PATIENCE*.

AAAAAAABLOMPHH
IT ALMOST FELT LIKE A VICTORY.
THEY'RE NOT INFALLIBLE. THEY'RE STILL THE... THE CHILDREN WE THINK, UNDER IT ALL.

I REMEMBER STIFLING THE URGE TO SHOUT OUT IN TRIUMPH AS HE DROWNED. TO STARE UP INTO THE HILLS-- SHE MUST'VE BEEN THERE, WATCHING--
--AND SCREAM YOU CAN'T HOLD THEM AAAAALL!

BUT THEY DIDN'T LOOK TO THE HILLS. THEY JUST SAT. AND TREMBLED, LIKE EVERY MUSCLE WANTED TO POUNCE AND ONLY THEIR TWANGING FUCKING BRAINS COULD STOP IT.
AND A HOOD WAS PULLED BACK AND A VOICE I HADN'T HEARD IN A LONG TIME SAID:

PRAAAAAAAIIISE.

P-PRAISE JESUS.
YOU FOUND CARMEL.
YOU FOUND CARMEL.

GOBACKGOBACKGOBACK AAAAND WWWWWWWWWWWWWWAITFORUSSSSSSSSS
OR NOW!?
OR NNNOW! HAHAH! YOU WANT IT NNNNOW?

COME IN.
COME IN.
GOD BLESS YOU BOTH. COME IN.

WE.
WE...

WE.
AYE.
AYE, I KNOW.
THEY DON'T CHASE US.
WE HAVE TO GO BACK.

THEY DON'T CHASE US AND THAT'S WORSE THAN IF THEY DID.

DETAILS.
HHH.
READY?
N...N--
BE READY.

DETAILS BARELY SEEM TO MATTER, DO THEY?
THE ACTS OF HEROISM. ACTS OF DESPERATION.
WAS THERE... WAS THERE PRIDE FOR OUR HOME, AS WE RETOOK IT?
MAYBE. MAYBE A BIT. BUT NOT REALLY.

MOSTLY IT'S JUST THAT WE HAD NOWHERE ELSE TO GO.
ACTS OF GENOCIDE. ACTS OF HORROR.
EDITH!
ACTS OF LOSS.
CHRISTINE!
WH... WHICH ONE IS IT?
...BUGGERED IF I KNOW.
HA.
HEH.
ACTS OF DISGUST. ACTS OF COURAGE.
LIKE LIMPETS, WE WERE. LIMPETS CLINGING TO A WALL TO SAVE OURSELVES FROM DANGER-- FORGETTING FOR JUST A MOMENT THE WALL WAS THE INSIDE OF A FUCKING SAUCEPAN.
THAT BEGUILING, INTOXICATING ILLUSION OF SANCTUARY.

REVEREND MOSES WHITE.
MO.
WOULD YOU LIKE SOME WHISKY?
GOOD START, MATE.
N'THANKS.
NOW OLD MO? HIS STORY WAS--
WELL ACTUALLY HIS STORY WAS PRETTY FUCKING BORING. AND HE TOLD IT WITHOUT RESERVATION OR REQUEST, WHICH TELLS YOU HE SIMPLY WASN'T RIGHT FOR WORLD 2.0.
THE CHURCH HAD A LITTLE CRÈCHE, Y'SEE? MY WIFE RAN IT.
A-AND ONE AFTERNOON... JUST AFTER HYMNS AND STORYTIME, THE MUMMIES AND DADDIES CAME TO COLLECT-- SAME AS EVERY DAY-- E-EXCEPT...
EXCEPT THE KNOCKING ON THE DOOR WAS... WAS A BIT LOUD. A-AND WHEN... WHEN MRS WHITE WENT TO OPEN IT...
ETCETERA ETCETERA. YOU KNOW. RAPE AND PILLAGE, DISASTROUS INTERVENTION OF LOCAL BOBBIES, TEN-MINUTE WINDOW TO SPIRIT AWAY THE TOTS.
BLOOD-SMEARED PEWS AND YADDA YADDA YADDA.

W... WE'VE BEEN HERE EVER SINCE.
OH, I MAKE LITTLE TRIPS OUT TO GET FOOD-- THERE'S PLENTY OF IT ABOUT-- BUT IT'S BEEN A TERRIBLE BURDEN. THAT'S HOW MOIRA HERE WANDERED OFF.
I THANK GOD YOU'VE COME.

SHIT STORY. GOOD WHISKY.
FAIR TRADE.
BRIEF STOPOVER, I THOUGHT. (IDIOT.) A NIGHT OR TWO TO REST AND RECOUP, THEN ONWARDS. NORTH: AS AGREED. NORTH WHERE IT'S COLD, WHERE IT'S SAFE.
WORST CASE SCENARIO, I THOUGHT? SHE'D TRY AND CONVINCE ME TO BRING THE KIDS TOO. I WAS READY FOR THAT. POINTS TO MAKE, ARGUMENTS TO EXTEND. BUT HELL, I KNEW HOW IT'D GO: SHE'D DO THAT THING-- IRON IN HER EYES-- TOTAL SHUTDOWN, AND THAT'D BE THAT.
SO MAYBE, I WAS THINKING, MAYBE WE COULD TAKE THEM? MAYBE I COULD THINK OF A WAY.
WORST CASE SCENARIO.

I WAS WRONG. STUPID FUCKING IDIOT. IT DRIPPED INTO MY BRAIN SLOWER THAN IT SHOULD.
NO AVOIDING IT. NO GETTING ROUND IT. THERE, WITH THEM, WITH A FUNCTION (JUST LIKE WHEN WE FOUND HER, WITH THOSE OLDIES)--

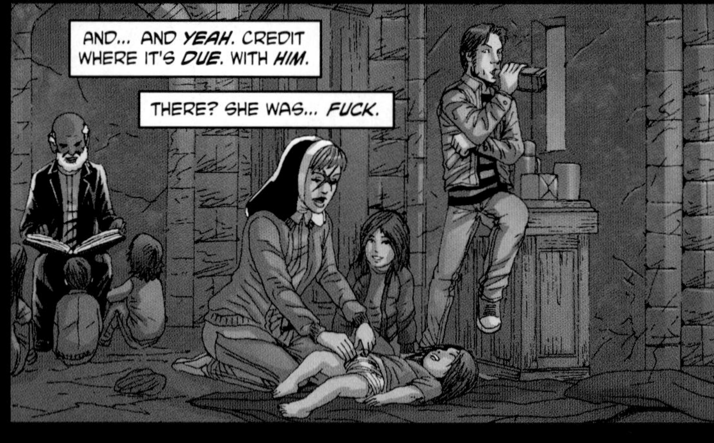
AND... AND YEAH. CREDIT WHERE IT'S DUE. WITH HIM.
THERE? SHE WAS... FUCK.

SHE WAS HAPPY.
WE NEED TO TALK.

SILENCE, DIARY. SILENCE IN THE AFTERGLOW.
THEY'RE OUT THERE. SHE'S OUT THERE.
WATCHING. GLARING. BUT NOT COMING.
SO IT SEEMS A PRETTY FUCKING SAFE BET SHE'S WAITING.
WE NEED TO TALK.
"CLAY LOAN," SELINE SAID. THAT LITTLE WHISPER FROM MY LOST LOVE. "TIME AND PLACE."
"EX."
Clay Loan
WELL WE KNOW WHERE AND WHAT "CLAY LOAN" IS NOW, DON'T WE DIARY, AND "EX" IS... IS PRESUMABLY ME? FOR FUCKSAKES.
"TIME AND PLACE."
SHE WANTS A FUCKING CHAT.
B-BALLS TO THAT.
BALLS TO THAT.

BUT THERE ARE LIGHTS TO THE WEST AT NIGHT. AND...

--AND NORTH, SO WE CAN CUT UP THROUGH THESE HILLS TO--
SHAKY.

...AND LIGHTS TO THE SOUTH.
LIGHTS TO THE FUCKING EAST.

AND DIARY? THE TRUTH IS AS UNAVOIDABLE AS PAIN. IT DOESN'T NEED TO BE SAID - BUT IT WILL BE.
STATING THE OBVIOUS IS WHAT YOU'RE ALL ABOUT.
WHAT THIS WORLD IS ALL ABOUT.

WE'RE FUCKIN' STUCK HERE.

I'M STAYING HERE.

ENTRY #WHO-THE-FUCK-KNOWS. I'VE LOST COUNT.
"TOGETHER WE STAND". THAT'S *BULLSHIT.*

YOU WANT TO KNOW THE MOST *HUMAN* THING OF ALL, DIARY? THE THING THAT *DEFINES* US? IT'S *THIS:*

UNDER *PRESSURE*... UNDER *STRAIN*... UNDER CIRCUMSTANCES WHERE *PATIENCE* AND *TEAMWORK* AND ALL THE FUCKING *REST* OF IT ARE THE *ONLY WAY* A *WHOLE GROUP* CAN PREVAIL...

...UNDER CIRCUMSTANCES WHERE *STRENGTH IN NUMBERS* REALLY IS THE *ONE* TRUE PATH?

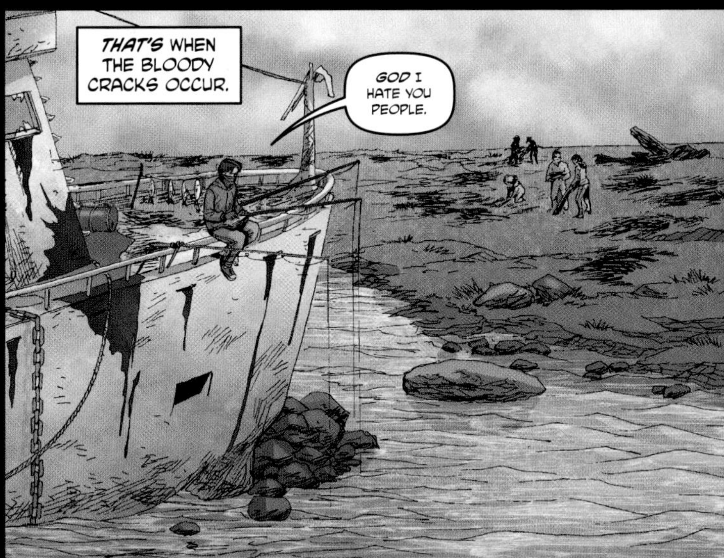

THAT'S WHEN THE BLOODY CRACKS OCCUR.
GOD I HATE YOU PEOPLE.

IT'S BEEN *DAYS*, DIARY. THE *SIEGE*-- ONLY WORD FOR IT-- IS *NOT* GOING *WELL*.

PLUSSIES LEFT US WITHOUT *FOOD*, WITHOUT *SHELTER*, WITHOUT *DEFENCE*. ROTTING *MEAT* EVERYWHERE. HOME SWEET TOXIC HOME.

STARTING FROM *SCRATCH*.
STARTING FROM *SCRATCH* WHEN WE *KNOW*... WE *KNOW* THEY'RE OUT THERE.
THE *SMART* ONES. THE *RESTRAINED* ONES. HER *ONES*. JUST WATCHING.

AND YOU *KNOW*, BECAUSE YOU CAN *SEE* IT.
THAT UNDER CIRCUMSTANCES LIKE *THIS?*
WE ALL STAND *ALONE*.

DIARY, LISTEN. WE DIDN'T EVEN KNOW THEY'D *GONE* UNTIL THEY CAME SLINKING *BACK*.

THERE WAS *ANGER* OF COURSE. AT THE *SNEAKINESS*, SO-CALLED. YOU ASK ME IT WAS JUST BECAUSE SKIP AND HIS FAMILY WERE THE FIRST WHO *TRIED* IT-- THE FIRST ONES *HONEST ENOUGH* TO *ABANDON SHIP*-- AND THE REST WERE SIMPLY *JEALOUS*.

THEY TOOK THE *ENGINE*. OFF TO GET THE *DAPHNE*. OFF TO SPEED AWAY ON THEIR OWN.

LOW.
HUH.
FUCKIN' *TREACHERY*, INNIT.
SO YEAH. ANGER, SURE. THOUGH MAYBE NOT AS MUCH AS YOU'D *THINK*.

YOU ONLY HAD TO *LOOK* AT THE POOR FUCKERS TO KNOW--
WH... WHERE'S *JACKIE*?

--KARMA ALREADY *HIT*.

STORY CAME OUT, BIT BY BIT. MOAN BY MOAN.
MUUUUUUUM.
WE WERE GONNA COME BACK FOR YA. WE WERE GONNA COME BACK FOR YA.
OR: ONE VERSION OF IT.

THEY SET OUT. (SNUCK OUT). THEY SAW SOME MOVEMENT.
LIGHTS IN THE DARK. MOVING. FOLLOWING.
THEY DECIDED.
WE... WE BLOODY PRESS ON, AWRIGHT?

KEEP THAT HAND ON THE TILLER, MATE.
CAN YA REACH IT, LOVE?
COURSE I CAN. I'M NOT FUCKING USELESS, YOU KN

AAA AAAA GO GO GO GO

Y-YOU.
WHAT'LL... WHAT'LL YER FUCKIN' NUN DO TO HER?
H... HOW SHOULD I KN--
IT'S NOT UP TO HER. NOT THIS SORTA THING.
... THE FUCK'S THAT MEAN?
GUYS? Y-YOU SHOULD... UH...
YOU NEED TO SEE THIS.
DO ME DO ME DO ME BETTER'N ANY FOOKIN' AUSSIE MAGGOTPRICK TEAR ME UP INSIDE DO MEEEEEE HA HA HA

WHAT CAN YOU *SAY?*

WHAT CAN YOU FUCKING *SAY,* DIARY?

AMEN.

HAHAHAHA I'M COMIIIIIIINNNNNGGGGG

DAD
DAD
DAD

...
...
...
I MET YER BLOODY MUM WHEN YOU WERE TWO. YER DAD WAS A JUNKIE CALLED TREVOR.
YOU GET THE FUCK AWAY FROM ME.

TOGETHER WE STAND.
TOGETHER WE STAND.
HH.
WE NEED TO TALK ABOUT THE ENVELOPE.

ENTRY #ONE-MORE-THAN-THE-LAST.
Y'KNOW... WE HAVEN'T SEEN ANY OF THE POOR THINGS IN *DAYS*.
I THINK MAYBE IT'S TIME TO GO FETCH MORE *FOOD*.
ENOUGH.
DIARY? *ENOUGH*.
SOMETIMES ALL THE *WAITING*, ALL THE *ROUTINE*, ALL THE *DREAR*... IT CAN'T *LAST*. THERE'S NO REASON. NO BUILDUP.
THERE'S A FLOWER OF SCOTLAND SHOP AWAY OVER THERE. WHERE D'YOU THINK I GET ALL THIS LOVELY BLOODY WHI--
NK
SIMPLY: *ENOUGH*.
OUR OLD FRIEND *CRITICAL MASS*. OVER AND OVER AND OVER.
ENOUGH. AND SOMEBODY HAS TO *DO SOMETHING* OR NOTHING WILL EVER *CHANGE*.
AND IT SEEMS, DIARY. IT SEEMS INSTEAD OF SAYING *"SOMEBODY SHOULD DO SOMETHING"*. IT SEEMS MAYBE I'M THE ONLY ONE WHO *CAN*.

BUGGER.
YOU SURE YOU WANT TO COME? LIKELIHOOD OF AN *ADMIRAL ACKBAR MOMENT*, 'N ALL THAT.
YOU WHAT?
DAD, PLEASE D--
SSHH.

YOU FUCKIN' STAY HERE.
CLAY LOAN.
EX.
TIME AND PLACE...

TIME. TO FACE THE MUSIC.
WE SHOULD KEEP HER QUIET, SHE'LL ATTRACT M--
IT'S FINE, LAD, IT'S FINE.
THERE WE GO, NO BOTHER, JUST HOLD HER FEET THERE...
NO TROUBLE, NO TROUBLE.
ENVY'S A FUNNY THING, DIARY.
COMES TO YOU AT THE STRANGEST FUCKING TIMES.
THEY WATCHED. STRAINING AT THEMSELVES.
PROMISED WHO-KNOWS-WHAT.
AND I WATCHED DES. BUNCHED, TIGHT-JAWED DES. FIRST-WITH-A-GUN DES. FIRST-TO-VOLUNTEER DESMOND OF THE ANGRY EYES.
SO FULL OF HATE. NOT AFRAID FOR ONE SECOND. NOT CONFUSED. NOT FUCKING DISTRACTED OR UNCERTAIN.
PROACTIVE. SIMPLE.
I LOOKED AT DES AND I WISHED I WAS HIM.

I... LORD... LORD, I ACHE ALL OVER.
C-CAN'T SLEEP.
THERE THERE, M'GIRL. IT'S OKAY.

HAVE A LITTLE DROP, EH? IT'LL HELP YOU GET OFF.
SHE DOESN'T DRINK.

PFFT. DOESN'T DRINK. AT A TIME LIKE THIS.
NOW LOOK HERE, YOUNG LADY, MY LOT MAY NOT AGREE WITH YOUR LOT ON A FEW THINGS, BUT ANGLICAN OR CATHOLIC IT'S A LOVING GOD WE'RE ABOUT.

IF YOU REALLY THINK HE'S THE SORT TO HOLD IT AGAINST YOU FOR... FOR SMOKING A CIGARETTE OR SAYING "FUCK", OR HAVING A WEE DRAM WHEN YOUR WHOLE BODY'S EXHAUSTED, THEN HE'S PROBABLY NOT WORTH ALL THE FUSS AFTER ALL-- EH?

I'D MADE THE SAME ARGUMENT A BILLION TIMES, DIARY.
SHE ALWAYS LAUGHED IT OFF.

KIRKWALL. *THEY* WATCHED. *I* WATCHED. WE *ALL* BLOODY *WATCHED.*
THREE TIMES I WAS SURE DES WAS ABOUT TO START SHOOTING. MORE *TENSE* THAN A *DYSLEXIC CAMPSITE.*

CLAY LOAN
THREE TIMES I WAS TORN BETWEEN *CALMING HIM DOWN* AND EGGING HIM *ON.* JOINING THE FUCK IN.
CLAY LOAN.
AND THREE TIMES HE THOUGHT BETTER OF IT ANYWAY.

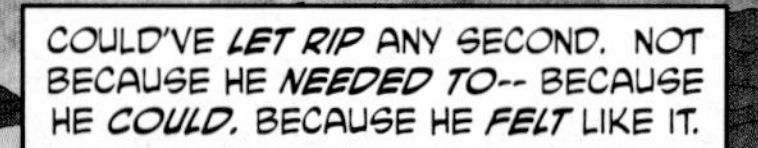
COULD'VE *LET RIP* ANY SECOND. NOT BECAUSE HE *NEEDED TO--* BECAUSE HE *COULD.* BECAUSE HE *FELT* LIKE IT.

EX.

"*TIME AND PLACE.*"
STANDING STONES OF STENNESS WHEN?

A-ALL *RIGHT*. ALL RIGHT, WELL...
I GUESS WE KNOW WHAT TO *DO*.
THIS IS FUCKIN' *WEIRD*, BRUV.

NOON?
HHH. NOON TOMORROW.
GIVE IT 'ERE.
SO... WHAT, DO WE JUST... JUST LEAVE IT HERE?
...
SORTA... SALTY.

SH.
SHAKY.
LISTEN. LISTEN-- I LOST MY SON INNA FIRST FUCKIN' DAYS OF ALL THIS.
WHAT?
OH GOD. OH GOD.
M.
MY BOOOOY.
I LEFT 'IM BEHIND. FUCKIN' RAN.
MY POOR ISAAC.

DES, WHAT'S WITH Y--
HHHHHATE.
YOU 'EAR ME? IT'S... IT'S FUCKING OVERWHELMIN'.
LIKE... REST OF YOU? I'VE SEEN, BRUV. BELIEVE. SURVIVAL. FEAR, INNIT? THAT'S WHAT DROWNS THE NOISE-- BUT ME?
I HATED.
HATED MYSELF FOR LOSING ONE KID. HATED THE OTHER ONE FOR SURVIVIN'. AND HATED EVERY FUCKIN' THING IN BETWEEN COS IT'S EASIER'N THINKIN'.
TRUTH IS.
FFFFFUCK.
T.
TRUTH IS.
STANDING STONES OF
OH NO.

TRUTH IS I'M LOOKIN' FORWARD TO THIS.

MY DAUGHTER.
HA.
T-TELL HER.
HA HA HA
TELL HER I LOVE 'ER.

"TELL HER I LOVE HER."

I'VE HEARD *WORSE*, AS FAR AS *LAST WORDS* GO.
DIARY.
DIARY, IT COULD BE... HA.
IT COULD BE THAT *THESE* ARE *MINE*.

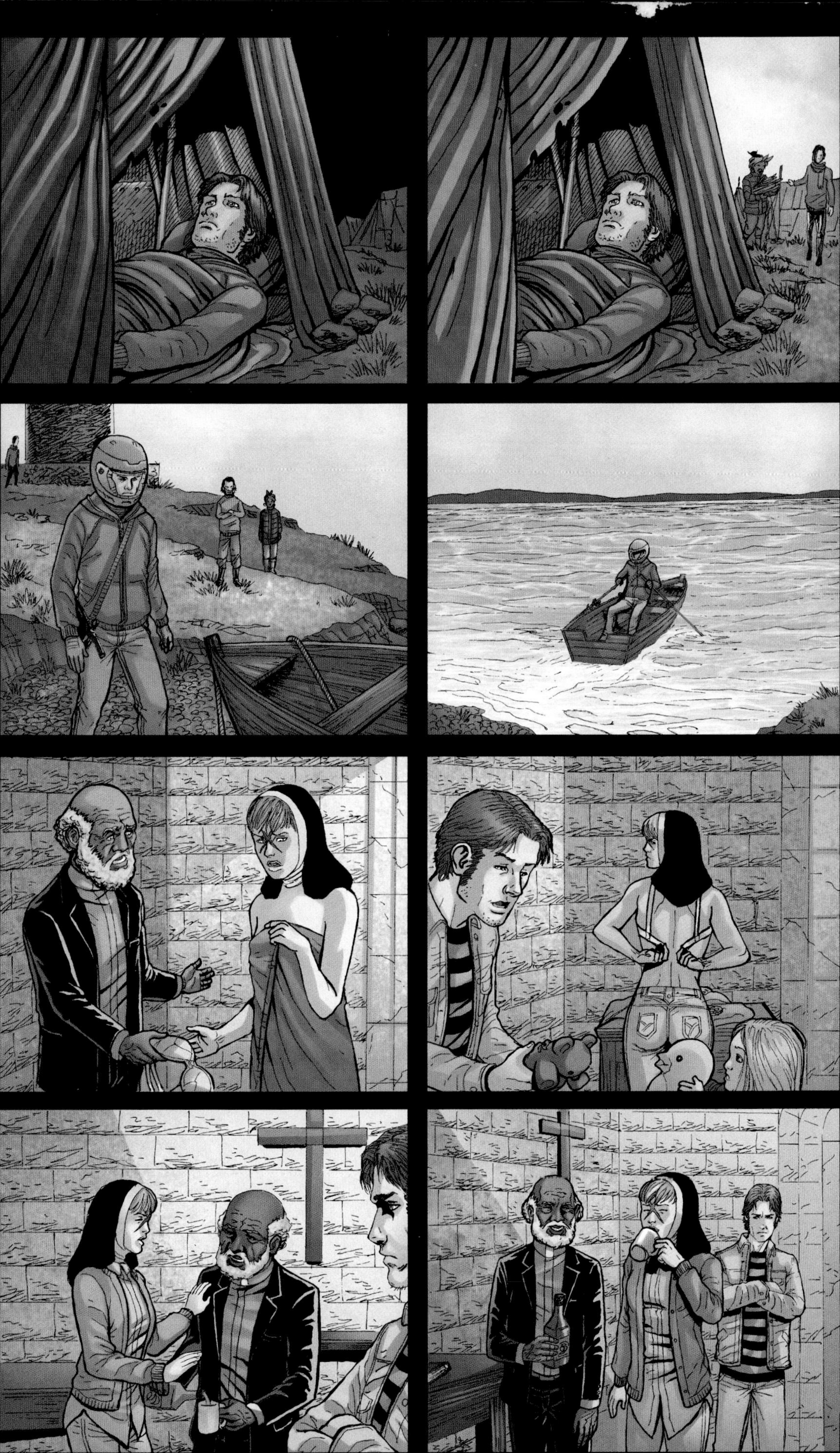

HELLO.
...
HUH.
POISONED *ENVELOPE* DIN'T WORK THEN.
SHE WAS *PROPER* PLEASED WITH 'ERSELF OVER *THAT* ONE.
...
WHO *IS* THIS?
DON'T BE *STUPID*, SHAKESPEARE.
YOU *KNOW* WHO.

IT WAS... *HARD GOING*, AT FIRST. THE *TALE*. THE *VOICE*.

OH, NOT JUST FOR THE *OBVIOUS*. CREEPING FINGERS OF *HATE AND HORROR* DOWN MY *NECK* LIKE *STORYTIME* WITH THE SHITTING DEVIL.

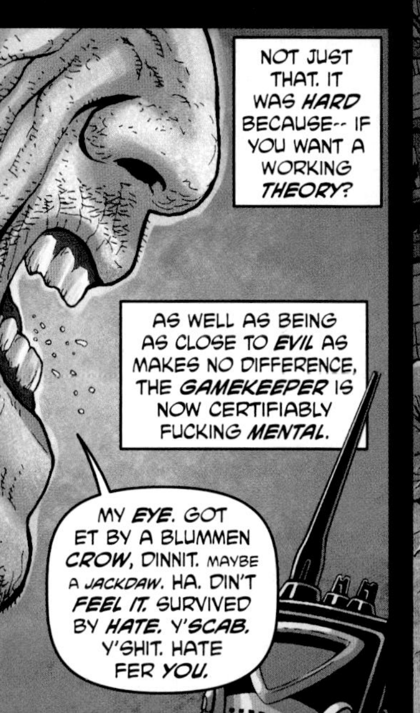
NOT JUST THAT. IT WAS *HARD* BECAUSE-- IF YOU WANT A WORKING *THEORY*?
AS WELL AS BEING AS CLOSE TO *EVIL* AS MAKES NO DIFFERENCE, THE *GAMEKEEPER* IS NOW CERTIFIABLY FUCKING *MENTAL*.
MY *EYE*. GOT ET BY A BLUMMEN *CROW*, DINNIT. MAYBE A JACKDAW. HA. DIN'T *FEEL IT*. SURVIVED BY *HATE*. Y'SCAB. Y'SHIT. HATE FER *YOU*.

ALARM WENT OFF ONCE AN HOUR, HE SAID, JUST LIKE I LEFT IT. *TWO DAYS* 'TIL THE *BATTERY DIED*. NO PLUSSIES. *"MIRACLE,"* HE SAID, LAUGHING.

ASHOKE FOUND HIM. POOR KID MUST'VE WANDERED FOR DAYS AFTER I... Y'KNOW. BACK THE WAY WE'D COME. THE *VOICE* JUST SAID:
TOOK THE PAKI *HOURS* TO PICK OUT ALL THE *SHOT*-- LITTLE *SPASTIC*.

DIFFICULT, DIARY. DIFFICULT TO *LISTEN*. DIFFICULT NOT TO *SPOUT QUESTIONS*, AND JUST AS TOUGH TO FORM A SINGLE BLOODY *WORD*.

HOW?
HOW DID YOU FIND *HER*?

HE JUST SAID:

PFT.

THEN:

TRACKED HER THROUGH TO *PERTH*, DINTWE? THAT *CHURCH*. THEM *KIDDIES*. HEH. WHAT *'APPENED* THERE, SHAKESPEARE?

YOU KNOW WHAT, DIARY? I STARTED TO FUCKING *TELL* HIM. STARTED TO *EXPLAIN*-- COULDN'T *STOP* MYSELF. EXCEPT. EXCEPT--

DON'T *BOTHER*. NOT *REALLY* INTERESTED. THIS ENT 'BOUT *ME* OR *YOU*, IZZIT? IT'S *HER*. SO HERE'S WHAT I *KNOW*:

SHE WENT *NORTH*. JOINED A *GROUP*.
STAYED *WEAK*. STAYED *USELESS*.
STAYED BLUMMEN *UNREMARKABLE*, IS WHAT.

THE CYCLE. YOU KNOW 'OW THEY ARE. GET 'EMSELVES SOME FUN, GO AT IT ALL AT ONCE.
NO HOLDIN' BACK. GO GO GO, KILL KILL KILL. FUCKEN ANIMALS.
AN' WHAT THEN BOY? EH? WHAT'S THEN IS TEDIUM. FER WEEKS AND WEEKS IN BETWEENTIMES.
H-HOW DO YOU KNOW ALL TH--
SHHH. MY STORY, Y'CUNT. HA. SHE TOLD ME. SHE TELLS ME, BOY.
NOW. NOW. WHAT HAPPENED, Y'SEE, WAS THIS. SHE WATCHED.
NOW. COME THE DAY 'ER PACK JOINED UP WITH THE SOLDIERBOYS. U.N. WALLAHS, THEY WERE - BLUE-BERET. EUROTRASH MOSTLY, THOUGH THEY SPEAK SOME QUEEN'S. 'CHOPPER CAME DOWN SOUTH OF AVIEMORE, BEEN SCHLEPPIN' ABOUT THE HIGHLANDS EVER SINCE.
AN' OF COURSE THEY'RE TOUGHER'N THE REST, SO SOON AS YOU LIKE IT THEY'RE THE TOP DOGS IN THE PACK. PLUSSIES BY THE DOZEN, OH YES-- AN' ALL AS BORED AS YOU LIKE.
'TIL THEY COME ACROSS THE CAMP.
(RIGHT THERE, DIARY. IT WAS RIGHT THERE THAT HIS VOICE WENT STICKY.)
NOW... BECAUSE SHE'S WEAK... BECAUSE SHE'S, HEH, SHE'S AT THE BACK. SHE'S GOT ALLA TIME INNA WORLD TO WATCH WHILE THE RESTA THEY BUGGERS GO HURTLIN' OFF.
(LIKE. LIKE HE WAS PROUD OF HER.)
AND SO SHE SEES WHAT NONE OF THEM OTHERS DO SEE.
(DOTING.)
AN' WHAT SHE SEES, MY BOY. HA. IS A TRAP.

WAIT.
'ERE, SHAKESPEARE. YOU WANT TO KNOW HOW IT STARTS? YOU WANT TO KNOW, HA, HOW YOU GET TO BE KING OF THE CROSSED? THE FIRST STEP? IT'S THIS.
YOU SHOUTS OUT AN ORDER. AN' YOU SEE WHICH OF 'EM'S GOT THE BRAIN TO PAY ATTENTION.
AN' THEN YOU GET RID OF ALL THE ONES WHO DON'T.
'COURSE IN 'ER CASE SHE DIN'T NEED THE LAST PART. TRAP DUNNIT FOR 'ER.
'AN IT WEREN'T LIKE THE ONES SHE SAVED WERE GRATEFUL. WEREN'T LIKE SHE COULD JUST TAKE CONTROL STRAIGHT OFF THE BAT.
SLOW. SLOWER.
D-DON'T DO IT ALL AT ONCE.
FACT IS THEY IGNORED 'ER. WEAKEST. WEIRDEST. QUIETEST. HENHH!
'BOUT ALL SHE'D ACHIEVED WAS SHOWIN' EM SHE DIN'T THINK THE SAME WAY, AN' SO FUCKEN WHAT?

SO YOU KNOW WHAT SHE DID, BOY? SAID THE SAME WORD OVER 'N OVER. THAT'S ALL. EVERY DAY WHILE THEY SHIVERED 'N SHAT.
BORING.
BORING.
HEH. THEY MUSTA BIN SICK OF THE SOUND OF 'ER.
SO NO BIG CHANGE. THEY MOVED ROUND. UP TH' HILLS, DOWN TH' DALES. SHE SAYS TO ME, BOY... SHE SAYS SHE CALLS IT THE DEAD TIME. HEH.
YOU EVER SEEN 'EM LIKE THAT?
THEY GO A WHILE WITHOUT FUN THEY GET SORTA... DREAMY. SPACED-OUT. LIKE THEY'RE ON PAUSE INNA BRAIN.
WEEKS, LAD. MONTHS MAYBE. FUCK KNOWS. SHE DUNT TELL ME 'OW LONG.
COMIN' 'ERE. LAUGHIN' AT ME. WHISPERIN' HER SHIT. THE CUNT. SORRY.
WAIT... SO... SO SHE COMES AND TALKS TO YOU QUITE OFTE--
ANYWAY. ONE DAY. ONE DAY COMES TH' CHANCE. PACK STUMBLES ACROSS SOME FUN, DUN'T THEY? AN' YOU KNOW WHAT SHE DOES, BOY?
REMEMBER!
BORING!
REMEMBER THE BOOOOORING!
GOSLOW!
NOTRUUUUUSH!
REMEMBER THE BORING BORING BORING BORING!

THE SECRET. THE SECRET. I'VE SEEN IT. Y'LITTLE SHIT. I'VE SEEN IT IN WAYS YOU ENT.
SHE MAKES 'EM THINK-- THAT'S ALL. NUTHIN' MAGIC. SAYS "NO" TO HERSELF AN' GETS THEM THINKIN' THE SAME.
'S ALL IT TAKES. YOU TELLS THE SMART ONES SOMETHIN' THEY DUNT KNOW AN' LET THEM WHITTLE-AWAY THE DUMMIES.
FUCKEN EVOLUTION, THAT.
T... TAKE TIME! MAKE IT LAAAST.
TAKE TIME.
NOTMORE BORING HAHA.
WAY SHE TOLD ME, MY BOY, THEY MADE THEM POOR FUCKERS IN THE BUS LAST TWO BLUMMEN WEEKS.
GAMES. TORTURES. SLOWFUN, Y'UNDERSTAND?
'COURSE THERE WAS... PRACTICALITIES TO ACCOUNT FER. CAN'T GO HANDLIN' THE MEAT IF YOU ENT INTENDING TO TURN IT, SO SHE COME-UP WITH THE SUIT. CLEVER CUNT. SORRY. SORRY. GLOVES 'N SOAP 'N WHATNOT.
AN' I DON'T THINK IT'S STRETCHIN' THE TRUTH, SHAKESPEARE, TO SAY THAT'S ABOUT WHEN ALL THEM BUGGERS WI' GUNS STARTED THINKIN' OF HER AS...
SSSSSSSSOMEONE COMING SOMEONE COMING MISSSSS
AS THE BOSS.
DIARY: THE VOICE IN THE RADIO WENT QUIET AT THAT. I THOUGHT-- NO, FUCK, I HOPED-- THE BATTERIES'D CARKED. BUT IT CAME HISSING BACK LIKE A SNAKE IN THE SUN AND WHAT IT SAID... WHAT IT SAID WAS:
THAT'S WHERE I COME IN.

I WAS STILL WEAK. BEEN TRACKIN' 'EM FOR A WHILE. S'POSE I WANTED... HHH. WANTED TO SEE YOU, IF I'M HONEST. SEE YOU WITH A CROSS. MAYBE KILL YOU.
I ASSUMED YOU WAS WITH 'ER.
SHE DIN'T LIKE THAT. NOT ONE BIT.
SSSSSSTOP
BUT THEY GOT THE PAKI STRAIGHT AWAY, DIN'T THEY? HIM SHOUTIN' "CUDDLES" LIKE A KIDDY. I 'MEMBER HER SCREAMIN' NO NO NO-- BUT THEY WAS TOO FIRED UP.
AN' ONE OF 'EM, BOY... THAT HAIRY WOG VICAR... HE COMES CRAWLING AT ME 'FORE I CAN GET OFFA SHOT AND HE BITES ME RIGHT IN THE LEG.
...
LEG OFF. BLOOD SQUIRTIN'. BUT IT'S 'ER SAYIN' "STOP" LIKE THAT I 'MEMBER MOST. HUH.
AN' THE WAY THEY ALL BLUMMEN DUN IT.
SO SHE PICKS UP ME LEG AND SHE TWATS THE WOG INNA FACE, AN' THE REST OF 'EM'RE STANDIN' THERE WATCHIN' AN' HOWLIN' AND HISSIN' - AN' YOU KNOW WHAT SHE GOES AN' DOES, SHAKESPEARE?
YOU KNOW WHAT SHE DOES RIGHT THEN AND THERE?

USE. USE. MAKE. ME. COME.
FIRST TIME I EVER SEEN PLUSSIES GO SILENT. PASSED OUT NOT LONG AFTER.
BUT I'M PRETTY SURE HIS HOLINESS DIN'T MANAGE IT.

THE VOICE. THE VOICE. THE VOICE.
SHE PUT ME IN THE *SUIT* AFTER THAT. BOUND UP THE LEG *'ERSELF*.
STRANGE TIME, SHAKESPEARE. MEMORIES'RE FUCKED. *CARRIED* SOME OF THE WAY, HOBBLED THE REST, ALL THEM *OTHER BUGGERS* EYEIN' ME UP. SURLY, LIKE. ONLY *HER* WORD TO KEEP 'EM *OFF*. HER WORD AND THE *PAKI*. YOU NEVER *SEEN* SUCH AN *OBEDIENT* LITTLE *PLUSSER*.
AN' THE *PRIEST?* OOOHHH, HIM WORST OF *ALL*. GLOWERIN' AN' *SEETHIN'*. LOST ALL HIS *STATUS*, HE HAD. WORSER'N A FUCKIN' *PET*.
ANYWAYS, THE ONE THING I *DID* KNOW FOR SURELY IS WHERE WE WAS *HEADED*--
CAVA.
--THOUGH I GOT NO BLUMMEN NOTION OF HOW SHE *KNEW* WHERE YOU *WAS*.

I... I DO.
IT WAS WHILE WE WERE IN *PERTH*. HOLED UP WITH THE... THE *VICAR*. I WENT OUT FOR A FAG. J-JUST STEPPED *OUTSIDE* AND--

A-ANYWAY, I COULDN'T GO WITH THEM, NOT STRAIGHT AWAY - I COULDN'T LEAVE HER-- SO--
BOY. *BOY*.
D'YOU *REALLY* THINK.
I GIVES A *SHIT?*

NO.
NO, OF COURSE HE DIDN'T. NOTHING TO SAY, DIARY. NOTHING FOR HIM TO LEARN. HE KNOWS THE SCORE. (FOR ALL I KNOW HE FUCKING WROTE IT.)
MYSTERIES, MYSTERIES, MYSTERIES. IGNORE, IGNORE, IGNORE.
NOW. THEM FIRST MONTHS INNA HILLS, MOSTLY ALL THEY DONE WAS WATCHIN'. SHE GOT 'EM RIGHT GOOD AT THAT. PEERIN' DOWN AT YOU LOT. SPYIN'.
YOU MOST OF ALL, Y'FUCK. Y'FFFFFFFUCK. HA.
WATCHING YOU AN' WATCHIN' YER REACTIONS.
EASY ENOUGH AT FIRST, WEREN'T IT? THEY UNDERSTOOD THE TAKE-IT-SLOW THING ALREADY. RESISTIN' 'EMSELVES. WAITIN'-FOR-FUN.
SHE GOT 'EM MAKIN' THEIR OWN BLUMMEN ENTERTAINMENT. GETTING THE LADS TO... TO CUT BITS OFFA THE WEAK PLUSSIES. MAKIN' THEM FUNNY SCULPTURES YOU SEEN...
SMART, THAT. KEEPIN' THE PISSY ONES CULLED AND THE OBEDIENT ONES INTERESTED.
MOSTLY IT WAS FOR THAT, ANYWAYS. SOMETIMES? HEH. I'LL GRANT YOU. SOMETIMES IT WAS TESTIN'. LITTLE TRAPS. WANTED TO SEE HOW SMART Y'WERE. HOW EASY IT'D BE TO DO YOU ALL WHEN THE TIME CAME.
BUT... YEAH.
MOSTLY IT WAS JUST TO SEE THE LOOK ON YER FACE.

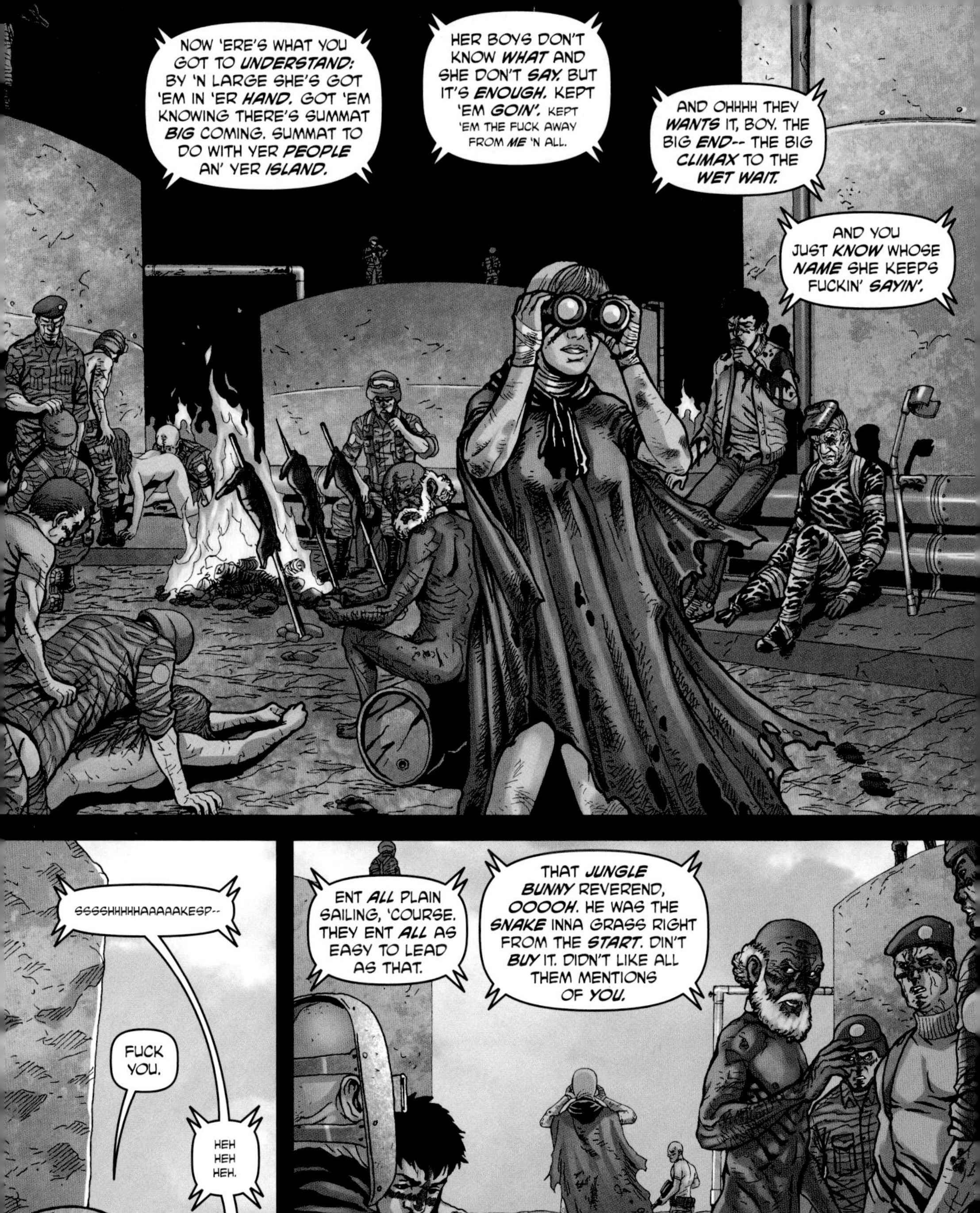
NOW 'ERE'S WHAT YOU GOT TO UNDERSTAND: BY 'N LARGE SHE'S GOT 'EM IN 'ER HAND. GOT 'EM KNOWING THERE'S SUMMAT BIG COMING. SUMMAT TO DO WITH YER PEOPLE AN' YER ISLAND.
HER BOYS DON'T KNOW WHAT AND SHE DON'T SAY. BUT IT'S ENOUGH. KEPT 'EM GOIN'. KEPT 'EM THE FUCK AWAY FROM ME 'N ALL.
AND OHHHH THEY WANTS IT, BOY. THE BIG END-- THE BIG CLIMAX TO THE WET WAIT.
AND YOU JUST KNOW WHOSE NAME SHE KEEPS FUCKIN' SAYIN'.

SSSSHHHHHAAAAAKESP--
FUCK YOU.
HEH HEH HEH.
ENT ALL PLAIN SAILING, 'COURSE. THEY ENT ALL AS EASY TO LEAD AS THAT.
THAT JUNGLE BUNNY REVEREND, OOOOH. HE WAS THE SNAKE INNA GRASS RIGHT FROM THE START. DIN'T BUY IT. DIDN'T LIKE ALL THEM MENTIONS OF YOU.
I DON'T S'POSE YOU'D CALL IT A REBELLION. NOT REALLY. I WAS THERE. I SAW IT, BOY.
THEY JUST SORT OF... BUILT UP. THEM ONES WHAT COULDN'T STAND IT BUBBLED OVER. LIKE FUCKIN' CHIMPS WINDIN' EACH OTHER UP.
BUNCH OF 'EM LEAPT T'THEIR FEET. STARTED SHOUTIN'. CAME FER ME.
AND YOU KNOW WHAT, SHAKESPEARE? HEH.

SHE WAS READY.
READY WITH 'ER BEST BOYS.

'ERE'S ONE FOR YOU. YOU EVER WONDERED WHY PLUSSIES DON'T KILL OTHER PLUSSIES?
MYSTERIES, MYSTERIES, MYS--
OH, THERE'S THE ODD BUMPOFF, RIGHT, FOR FOOD OR WHATNOT. BUT ENT OFTEN FOR FUN. KNOW WHY?
IGNORE, IGNORE, IGN--
WELL I'LL TELL YOU.

THEY DON'T SCREAM, BOY. LAUGH TOO MUCH. SIMPLE AS THAT. SADIST'S WORST FUCKEN NIGHTMARE'S A FELLER WHO ENJOYS IT.
EXCEPT. HEH. EXCEPT SHE'S BRIGHTER'N THAT, ENT SHE?
SO SHE UP'N SHE CONVINCED 'EM. MADE 'EM TAKE PLEASURE IN IT.
NOT BECAUSE IT'S FUN, YOU UNDERSTAND? BUT BECAUSE IT MEANS YOU'RE FUCKEN BETTER 'N THE ONE YOU DONE FOR.
AND TO SHOW IT, SHAKESPEARE? YOU SHIT. YOU FFFFUCKEN LITTLE... HRRR... T-TO SHOW IT...? SHE HAD 'EM CARVE A BLUMMEN GREAT "X" ONTO THEM WHAT SHE'D BEATEN.

SO THAT TIDED 'EM OVER A WHILE. FRESH DIVERSIONS, LIKE.
KEPT 'EM... KEPT 'EM LEAN, I S'POSE. WEEDED OUT THEM ONES WHAT GOT NO DISCIPLINE. HUNTED NEWBIES WHEN THEY COULD - USE 'EM AS ALARMS. CHAINED-UP, KEPT FED. LIVING BLUMMEN MOTION DETECTORS.
MAKIN' USE OF THEM ONES WHAT COULDN'T TAKE THE PACE.
THEM ONES WHAT... HHH... WHAT DIDN'T ADORE HER.
AND OH, OHHHHH FUCK DIARY. YOU COULD HEAR IT, AFTER THAT. YOU COULD HEAR IT IN EVERY SICKLY WORD HE SAID.
...
YOU LOVE HER.
WHAT YOU SAY?
I. I S--
DON'T CARE. SSSH. ANYWAY. ANYWAY ANYWAY ANYWAY LISTEN.
HE'S MAD. SAID IT WAS... WAS ALL MY FAULT. SAID I'D FUCKED IT UP YET AGAIN.
BUGGERIN' OFF TO THE MAINLAND LIKE THAT.
THE SORTIE. HE MEANT THE SORTIE. THE SORTIE SHAT ON EVERYTHING.
NEVER SEEN HER SO FIRED UP. PANICKIN' YOU WAS OFF FOR GOOD.
HE SOUNDED...
DIARY. LISTEN. OH GOD.
HE SOUNDED JEALOUS.

'COURSE, OUR OLD PAL HIS HOLINESS WAS STILL UP TO HIS SHIT. SNEAKY WOG CUNT PERSUADED SOME OF THE LADS TO OPEN UP WI' THE MORTARS.
FUCKED THAT UP, DIN'T THEY? HEH.
BLUMMEN FURIOUS, SHE WAS. NO SENSE TO WHY SHE LETS HIM GET AWAY WITH IT, THE FUCK.
GOT ISSUES WITH TYIN' UP LOOSE ENDS, POOR COW. THAT'S MY BET. HEHHN.
S'POSE YOU REMEMBER THE NEXT PART YERSELF. OHHH, SHE TOLD ME ALLA BOUT THAT. FOLLOWED YER BOAT. KEPT 'ER DISTANCE.
W-WE LOST THEM. WE GOT AWAY.
BALLS. SHE LET YOU GET CLEAR SO'S SHE'D KNOW WHERE YOU WAS HEADIN'. COME BACK THE NEXT MORNIN' KNOWIN' WELL AND SURE WHERE YOU SET DOWN.
I THINK... I THINK THE VOICE BROKE AGAIN THERE, DIARY. A WOBBLE. HE SAID SHE PUT ASHOKE IN THE WRAPPERS. HER FUCKWITTED LITTLE ROBOT.
SHE SENT HIM OFF TO FOLLOW, TO KEEP TABS, TO BRING ME BACK IF HE COULD... AND SHE LEFT THE WITHERED OLD FUCK WITHOUT HIS SUIT OR HIS GUARD.
AND OH, THE VOICE BREATHED. CRACKLED DOWN THE LINE. AND SAID:
YOU KNOW WHAT I THINK, SHAKESPEARE?
I THINK.
THAT SHE THINKS.
YOU'RE GOD.

DIARY? *THROUGHOUT.* THROUGHOUT *ALL* OF IT... ALL I *WANTED* TO SAY WAS *WAIT. STOP.*

ACTUALLY WHAT I WANTED WAS TO THROW DOWN THE *RADIO* AND *RUN* AND GO *HOME* AND BURY MY HEAD AND *SLEEP FOREVER* BUT.

WHAT D'YOU MEAN? WHAT D'YOU MEAN SHE THINKS I'M GOD?
SSSHH. MY STORY. NO QUESTIONS. BATTERIES WON'T LAST FOREVER.
NOW. THERE WAS TWO EPISODES OF SHITBAGGERY WHILE YOU WAS AWAY, AN' THEY WAS BOTH YOUR FAULT. FIRST WAS - WHAT WITH THE PAKI GALAVANTIN' OFF AFTER YOU IN HIS FUCKEN BINBAG--

BUT THERE IS NO FUCKING RUNNING, THERE IS NO SLEEP, THERE'S NO *HOME* TO GO TO AND ALL THAT MATTERS, IN ORDER TO STAY ALIVE, IS THAT SPLENDID OLD MANTRA:

MYSTERIES MYSTERIES MYSTERIES, IGNORE IGNORE IGNORE.

BUT I ASKED THE FUCKING *QUESTION* ANYWAY.

--THERE WAS NO SOD TO LOOK OUT FOR YOURS TRULY.

CUNT OFF!

ARSEFUCK.

RRRRRRRRR
NOW BEFORE YOU ASK--
I WASN'T GOING T--
--I DON'T RIGHTLY KNOW WHY I DONE THAT. CARVED THE X. IT'S... IT'S LIKE I SAID: MOSTLY SHE DONE THAT TO THEM BUGGERS SHE'D BEATEN. OR AT LEAST SHE 'AD HER BOYS DO IT FOR HER.
M. MAYBE THAT'S WHY, THEN. MAYBE THAT MADE ME HERS.
WHATEVER FUCKEN REASON, OUTCOME'S A RIGHT OLD LAUGH. SHE SAYS - NOWADAYS, I MEAN, WHEN SHE COMES TO CHAT--
...SHE SAYS THEM OTHERS, HA. THEY THINK I'M SOME SORTA BOGEYMAN. SOMETHIN' SPECIAL, LURKIN' OUT HERE. SOMETHIN' TO BE AVOIDED AT NIGHT.
HAHA.
"A CROSSED," THE VOICE WHISPERED.
"A CROSSED WITHOUT A CROSS.
"THAT'S WHAT THEY THINK I AM."
ANYWAYS. SOON AS SHE FOUND US SHE DONE THE SAME WITH ME HAND SHE DONE WITH ME LEG.
PUT ME IN MY PLACE, MAYBE. AN' THE WOG. PETS 'N FUCKEN SLAVES, THE BITCH. SORRY. SHOWS OF SENIORITY. BUT IF YOU WANT MY THEORY, HA, IT'S MORE'N THAT.
IT'S LIKE A WAY OF SAYIN', TO THEM OTHERS, YOU CAN HAVE FUN WITH THE PREY WITHOUT KILLIN' IT. WITHOUT TURNIN' IT.
MAKES 'EM THINK. THAT'S ALL SHE EVER BLUMMEN DOES. ALL SHE BLUMMEN NEEDS TO.
TOLD YOU THERE WAS TWO THINGS 'APPENED WHILE YOU WAS GONE, DIN'T I? SECOND ONE WAS A FEW DAYS AFTER. WENT SUMMAT LIKE:
IS IT HIM? HE'S BACK? HE'S BACK?

MADE ME COME ALONG, DIN'T SHE? BOAT OF OUR OWN, SNEAKIN' OUT TO HOY. HER IN A BLUMMEN HELMET.
"WANT YOU THERE," SHE KEPT SAYIN'. "IF IT'S HIM. DON'T WANT HIM TO RUN. JUST IN CASE IT'S HIM."
Y'FUCKEN TEACHER'S PET.
TAKE.
TAKE SLOW.
SLOWFUN.
SAVELEADER.
IT WEREN'T YOU, OF COURSE.
Y'KNOW... YOU PRICKS'RE FUCKIN' LUCKY I FOUND YOU. I GOT CONCRETE EVIDENCE OF A SAFE HAVEN RIGHT OVER THERE ON CAVA, COURTESY OF A SHIT I HAPPENED TO MEET, AND IN THE MORNIN' I'LL SHIP YOU OVER AND PROVE IT.
AND YET, OHHH YOU FUCKS, STILL YOU GOT TO QUIBBLE OVER WHO GETS THE LAST CAN OF BEANS.
CUNTS, THE LOTTA Y--
YOU.
I DO WONDER. I DO WONDER.
WAS SHE HOPIN' IT WAS YOU, SHAKESPEARE? DID SHE STOP THERE FOR A WHILE LIKE THAT JUST TO PRETEND TO 'ERSELF? TO, HEHHN. TO FUCKEN PLAY ACT?

I.
I SHIT MESELF. OH.
S-SORRY. SORRY, I. I DONE A SHIT.
YOU GOT TO IMAGINE IT, LAD. ALL THAT CARNAGE GOIN' ON ROUND 'ER. ALL THAT CRUELTY.
SHE DONE GIVE 'ER BOYS A PARTY AN' STOOD THERE INNA MIDDLE, AND WHAT YOU GOT TO UNDERSTAND IS: THERE'S NOT A PLUSSER INNA WORLD COULD'VE STOPPED 'EMSELVES TEARING THAT GINGER FUCKHEAD A NEW HOLE.
ALL THEM SCREAMS. SOUNDSA MURDER. SMELLA SEX. JUICES FLOWIN'.
NOT A ONE.
GO.
AWAY.
THE MAN RAN, THE RADIO SAID. THE MAN RAN AND THE SOLDIERS GAPED.
SHE'D DONE SHOWED 'EM ALREADY-- THERE'S JOY IN BEIN' STRONGER.
SO THEY UNDERSTOOD, DIN'T THEY?
...THAT THERE'S NEVER BEEN ONE AS STRONG AS HER.
CROWNED HER NOT LONG AFTER. OTHERS STARTED TAKIN' THE X-- VOLUNTARY, LIKE. MEANING: BEATEN. YOU UNDERSTAND THE... THE FUCKEN SYMBOLISM, BOY? COS THEY DID. THEY DO.
'COURSE I DIN'T SEE NONE OF IT. SHE 'AD ME SET UP DOWN 'ERE IN ME CAVE BY THEN. OWN SAFETY, I S'POSE.
BUT I HEARD, BOY. I HEARD ALL ABOUT IT.
DIARY. DIARY, I LISTENED TO MYSELF WHISPER INTO THAT RADIO. WHISPER SO QUIET I WASN'T SURE HE'D HEAR. I ASKED HIM... I ASKED HIM ABOUT WHEN HE TALKS TO HER... WHEN SHE COMES TO SEE HIM.
I SAID: WHAT'S SHE LIKE? (MY POOR LOVE.)
HE JUST LAUGHED AND CARRIED-ON.
SHE TOLE' ME YOU'D COME 'OME, NOT LONG AFTER. SAID THE PAKI BRUNG A LETTER. HEH HEH, Y'SOPPY CUNT. WEAK, THAT. WEAK, SHAKESPEARE.
PAKI BRUNG A PRISONER TOO. FAT YANK BIRD. AN' A BOX OF AMMO.
AND SO SHE LOOKS AT ME, M'BOY-- THE X LADY. THE BIIIITCH. SORRY. SHE LOOKS AT ME AFTER YER 'OME AGAIN AND SHE SAYS: "WHAT SHOULD I DO, MR TOOLEY?"

...
WHAT DID YOU TELL H
I ASKED HER WHAT SHE WANTED. ABOVE ALL ELSE. KNOW WHAT SHE SAID?
"THE END."
PFFT. SO I TOLD HER TO STOP DANCING ROUND THE FUCKEN MIDDLE AND DO SOMMAT ABOUT IT.
IF.
HHH.
IF YOU WANT THE TRUTH, BOY... I WAS SORTA HOPIN' SHE'D KILL ME AN' BE DONE WITH IT. HOPIN' I WAS THE END SHE WANTED.
THAT SAME FUCKEN DAY SHE TOOK TO PREPPIN' FOR SENDING A MESSAGE. RECKON THAT THERE LETTER OF YOURS GIVE 'ER THE IDEA.
BULLYIN' THE FAT YANK. BREAKIN' HER MIND. INSTRUCTIONS. CLAY LOAN. ALL THAT.
LEFT THAT SHITTY AMMO ONNA BEACH TO BE FOUND 'N ALL.
TESTING. TESTING, LIKE ALWAYS. WATCHIN' FOR THE LOOK ON YER FACE.
BANGHAHA HEAR BANG.
CUDDLES.
WE GETTIM? HE DEAD SNAKEY SHIT LITTLE NOTHING?
NO.
NOT HURT.
THANK GOD.

NEXT DAY... NEXT DAY YOU 'AD A LITTLE FACE TO FACE, DIN'T YOU? BLEW UP THE FUCKEN' GINGER CUNT. YOU KNOW WHAT SHE TOLD 'EM ALL, SHAKESPEARE, BEFORE THEY WENT OUT THERE TO WATCH? HENH.
"ANYONE WHO HURTS THAT MAN," SHE SAYS-- MEANIN' YOU, Y'FFFFFFUCK-- "WON'T BE A PART OF THE BIG FUN." AN' OF COURSE THEY TAKES IT IN AND DOES WHAT SHE SAYS, BUT OOOOOH YOU CAN SEE.
THEY WEREN'T HAPPY.
NOPE, IT ENT A LIE M'BOY, TO SAY 'ER STAR STARTED TO FADE AFTER YOU COME BACK. THEM OTHER LADS SCOWLIN'. THE WOG WHISPERIN' ...
SHE'D GOT THE YANK. SHE'D GOT ME OUT 'ERE. NOT LONG 'FORE THEY STARTED WONDERIN' IF SHE WAS SICK. SOFT. NOT STRONG NO MORE. STARTED TO WONDER IF SHE WAS REALLY IN IT FOR THE FUN AT ALL.
SO SHE UPS, BLESS 'ER HATEFUL FUCKEN HEART, AN' SHE MAKES 'EM THE ONLY PROMISE SHE EVER DID.
GREAT. BIG AND WONDROUS THINGS COMING. HAH. BIGFUN. NO MORE BORING. NO MORE BORING FOR MY BOYS.
SOON. SOON. WORTH. THE. WAIT.
DIARY: THE VOICE IN THE RADIO SAID, "I DO BELIEVE I CAUGHT HER PRAYING ONCE OR TWICE AFTER THAT." THEN IT GIGGLED. GIGGLED AND HISSED:
AND MAYBE THAT'S ALL THE PROOF YOU NEEDED, SHAKESPEARE, THAT THE ALMIGHTY ENT ON OUR SIDE NO MORE--

'CUS SHE GOT WHAT SHE BLUMMEN WANTED.

SO.
SO. SO THE VOICE CRACKED HARDER... SOMETHING LIKE... LIKE A SOB. THE SKY SHIFTED, THE SUN FELL, THE WORLD DIED AGAIN AND AGAIN. IT WAS... A WEIRD FUCKING DAY, DIARY.
SO YOU KNOW MOST OF WHAT HAPPENED AFTER THAT. WATCHIN' THEM YANKS ONNA FLEET. THE ENVELOPE BUSINESS. PASSIN' OFF THE FAT LASS TO THE MADMAN.
HEH. SHE DIN'T TELL ME 'BOUT THE DRIED CROSSPISS ONNA ENVELOPE STRIP, MIND, 'TILL AFTER IT WAS GONE.
SNEAKY BITCH. SORRY.
WHY DO YOU KEEP APOLOGISING WHENEVER YOU CALL HER A B--
EEEEEEEEEEB WRONG QUESTION.

...
DOES... DOES SHE WANT ME TURNED? OR DEAD? OR... OR WHAT?
AH.
NOW THAT'S MORE LIKE IT.

OHHHHH LORD I DO 'OPE SHE WANTS YOU TURNED. FUCKED-UP AS BAD AS THE REST. I DO PRAY THAT'S WHAT'S AT THE END. HH.
NOT SOME EASY LITTLE DEATH FOR YOU.

HE SPEEDS UP DIARY. RUSHING NOW. RUSHING FOR THE END THAT HASN'T COME. RUSHING EVEN THOUGH ALL HE'S GOT TO TALK ABOUT IS--

NOTHING WAS CHANGIN', WAS IT? JUST LIKE BACK AT THE START. THEM GAPS BETWEEN ATTACKS. THE DEAD TIME.
EXCEPT BACK THEN IT WAS 'ER RAILING AGAINST IT, WEREN'T IT? MARKIN' IT OUT-- "BORING, BORING", ALL THAT. MAKIN' SURE THEY 'MEMBERED IT.
WELL THEY DID. ONLY THIS TIME IT WAS 'ER FAULT FROM TOP TO BOTTOM.
SHE TRIED HER BEST, POOR THING. PROMISES OF BIGGER THINGS. THE BIG FINALE. WOULDN'T LET 'EM OFF AFTER THE YANKS INNA BOATS. "NOT YET," SHE KEPT SAYIN'. "SOON."
GOT DESPERATE NOW AND THEN. I SEEN IT. STARTS WAFFLIN' ON ABOUT YOU. Y'TWAT. Y'CUNT. THAT'S WHEN SHE LOSES 'EM THE WORST.
NOW... THE WOG? HIS-BLEEDIN'-HOLINESS? HE'S GETTIN' STRONGER THAN EVER. WHISPERIN'. LOOKIN' FOR CRACKS.
OHHH, SHE WON'T PUT HIM DOWN THE WAY HE DESERVES - AND MAYBE YOU KNOW THE REASON FOR THAT, SHAKESPEARE, CUS I FUCKEN DUNT. BUT IT WAS OKAY. Y'UNDERSTAND?
SHE COULD MANAGE, LONG AS SHE 'AD HER PET PAKI TO WATCH 'ER BACK.

AND THEN YOU.
NO, WAIT, DIARY, IT WASN'T ME--
YOU AGAIN.
I MEAN OKAY, MAYBE I POINTED THE TARGET OUT TO JACKSON, BUT--
ALWAYS. FUCKEN. YOU.

HIS HOLINESS TOOK THE OPPORTUNITY. I DOUBT SHE DONE MUCH TO STOP HIM. WAVED 'EM ALL OFF, EVEN.
WHATEVER SHE IS, BOY. HOWEVER DIFFERENT. HOWEVER SPECIAL.
SO SPECIAL.
EVERYONE'S GOT A LIMIT.

MORTARED 'EM FROM THE BEACH. COVERED EACH OTHER WHILE THEY WENT UP THE ROPES.
CRAZY 'N OUT-OF-CONTROL 'N FUCKEN MENTAL THEY MIGHT'VE BIN, BUT STILL. FUCKEN SOLDIERS, BOY.
THEM YANKS DIN'T 'AVE A CHANCE.
I IMAGINE SHE GOT 'ERSELF BACK TOGETHER PRETTY QUICK. MADE THE BEST OF A BAD JOB. FIGURED A WAY TO TURN IT TO 'ER ADVANTAGE.
BUT YOU COULD 'EAR, BOY. WHEN SHE SPOKE, NOT LONG AFTER. WHEN SHE COME TO ME. YOU COULD 'EAR IT IN 'ER VOICE.
SHE'D LOST CONTROL. FOR JUST A SECOND. JUST A MINUTE. AND IT SHOOK HER LIKE NOTHIN' ELSE.

THE RADIO SAID SHE MADE SURE TO INSTRUCT HER *CORE GROUP*. "HER *BOYS*," IT SAID, AND *SPAT*.

SHE TOLD THEM TO TAKE AS MANY *WEAPONS* AS THEY COULD. LEAVE THE *YANKS* UNARMED. SHE *KNEW* WHAT'D HAPPEN-- WHAT THE *NEWLY CROSSED* WOULD DO. NO DISCIPLINE THERE. NO OBEDIENCE.

SHE KNEW SHE COULDN'T *STOP THEM*.

SO SHE LET 'EM GO, SHAKESPEARE. LET 'EM GO AND... ROLL OVER YER FUCKEN ISLAND LIKE A WAVE. KNEW IT WOULDN'T KILL YOU. KNEW IT WOULDN'T BEAT YOU.
A BLOODLETTING. WAY TO... TO BLOW OFF SOME STEAM. WEAKEN YOU PRICKHEADS ALL THE MORE. FORCE YOU TO COME CHAT LIKE THIS.

ANYWAY. SHE BRUNG ME FOOD THAT NIGHT. AFTER THEY TURNED THE YANKS. BEFORE THE SHIP CAME FOR YER ISLAND.
BROKEN DOWN, SHE WAS. CAME AS CLOSE TO KILLIN' ME AS EVER, THERE. ALL OVER A FUCKEN SPASTIC-BRAINED PAKI. ≑TT≑. THEN SHE JUST WALKED OFF WITHOUT ANOTHER WORD.
I.
I KNOW.

I WAS THERE.
HEHN. WONDERED AS MUCH.
FOUND A PEN UP THE WAYS FROM 'ERE. PUT ME IN MIND OF YOU AN' THEM SOPPY LETTERS. HEHN.
SHOULD'VE KILLED ME WHEN YOU 'AD THE CHANCE, Y'DAFT FUCK.
DIARY, STOP.
STOP THE CLOCK AND HOLD THE FRONT PAGE AND FOR FUCK'S SAKE LISTEN. LISTEN TO WHAT DIDN'T HAPPEN WHEN HE DROPPED HIS LIMP LITTLE THREAT.
MY SPINE, DIARY.
MY SPINE DID NOT TINGLE.
JUST.
JUST FINISH THE BLOODY STORY, WILL YOU?
NF.
HIS HOLINESS. THE GOD-WOG. HE SHOWED THE LADS HE COULD BRING THE FUN, SO BEFORE YOU KNOW IT HE'S UP ON THE SAME PEDESTAL AS HER. A THREAT, BOY.
SO SHE'S SMART. SHE GIVES 'IM A JOB. "KEEP THEM ON THE ISLAND," SHE SAYS.
BEAUTY OF IT IS, IF HE DONE IT RIGHT HE'S STILL HER SLAVE. AND IF HE FUCKS IT UP ONE OF YOUR LOT'D PROBLY KILL 'IM. WIN-WIN.
OHHH I BET HE CAME CLOSE, DIN'T HE? CLOSE TO LOSIN' HIS GRIP. GOIN' FOR IT.
ORR NNNOW? HAHAHA! YOU WANT IT NNNNOW?
ALWAYS ITCHING, THAT ONE. ALWAYS PUSHING.
BUT THEY'D 'AD THEIR FUN AN' THE SHIT SHE TAUGHT 'EM GOES DEEP. THE WAIT-FOR-IT. THE CONTROL. SO MAYBE HIS HOLINESS LOST HIS NERVE. MAYBE SHE'S STILL GOT A HOLD OVER HIM 'N ALL.
OR MAYBE THE FUCKER'S JUST AS BRIGHT AS SHE IS AN' HE'S GOT HIS OWN SCHEMES.

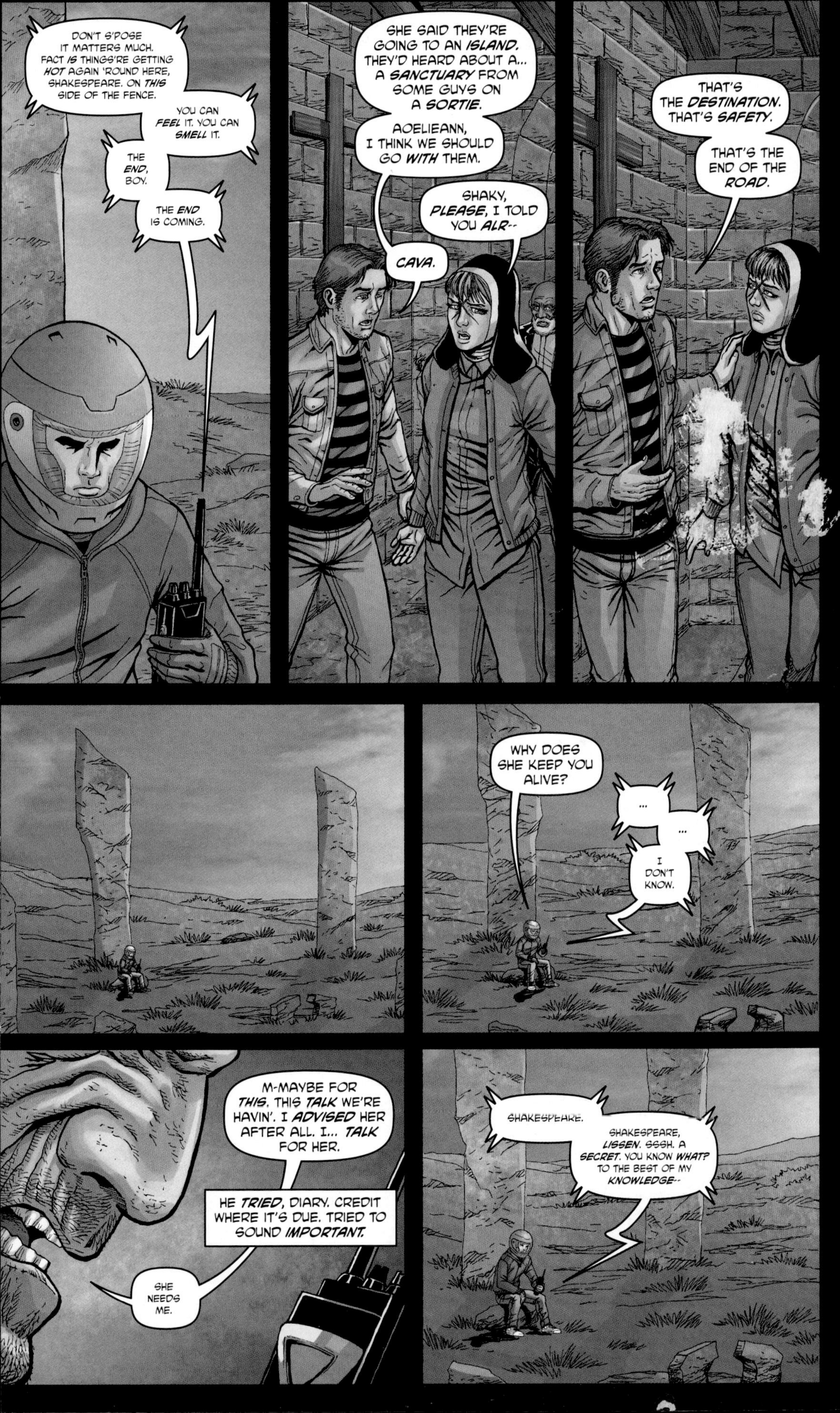
DON'T S'POSE IT MATTERS MUCH. FACT *IS* THINGS'RE GETTING *HOT* AGAIN 'ROUND HERE, SHAKESPEARE. ON *THIS* SIDE OF THE FENCE.
YOU CAN *FEEL* IT. YOU CAN *SMELL* IT.
THE *END*, BOY.
THE *END* IS COMING.
SHE SAID THEY'RE GOING TO AN *ISLAND*. THEY'D HEARD ABOUT A... A *SANCTUARY* FROM SOME GUYS ON A *SORTIE*.
AOELIEANN, I THINK WE SHOULD GO *WITH* THEM.
SHAKY, *PLEASE*, I TOLD YOU *ALR*--
CAVA.
THAT'S THE *DESTINATION*. THAT'S *SAFETY*.
THAT'S THE END OF THE *ROAD*.
WHY DOES SHE KEEP YOU ALIVE?
...
...
I DON'T KNOW.
M-MAYBE FOR *THIS*. THIS *TALK* WE'RE HAVIN'. I *ADVISED* HER AFTER ALL. I... *TALK* FOR HER.
HE *TRIED*, DIARY. CREDIT WHERE IT'S DUE. TRIED TO SOUND *IMPORTANT*.
SHE NEEDS ME.
SHAKESPEARE.
SHAKESPEARE, *LISSEN*. SSSH. A *SECRET*. YOU KNOW *WHAT*? TO THE BEST OF MY *KNOWLEDGE*--

HERE'S THE THING, DIARY.

YOU... YOU PEEK BEHIND THE CURTAIN. THE THINGS YOU'VE SPENT SO MUCH TIME AVOIDING. THE MYSTERIES YOU IGNORED. YOU TURN TO LOOK AT LAST AND YOU EXPECT, WHAT? GREAT HORRORS. GREAT SECRETS.

BUT YOU DON'T GET THEM. YOU GET PEOPLE BEING PEOPLE. PETTY AND MUNDANE. SELF-AGGRANDISING. INFLATING THEIR OWN FUCKING IMPORTANCE AT ANY COST.

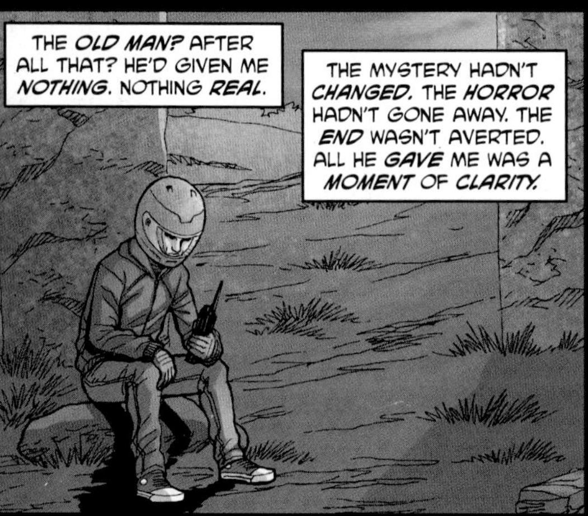

THE OLD MAN? AFTER ALL THAT? HE'D GIVEN ME NOTHING. NOTHING REAL.
THE MYSTERY HADN'T CHANGED. THE HORROR HADN'T GONE AWAY. THE END WASN'T AVERTED. ALL HE GAVE ME WAS A MOMENT OF CLARITY.

MR TOOLEY. G-GAMEKEEPER.
I WANT YOU TO KNOW.

I'M NOT AFRAID OF YOU ANY MORE.

...
...
ARE YOU STILL THERE?
HELLO?

AND A VOICE, DIARY.

NOT HIS.

NOT HIS.

A VOICE SAID:

GO HOME, SHAKESPEARE.
THEY'RE COMING. BEEN WATCHING YOU.

DUSK.
TOLD THEM. TIME TO COME. SEND YOU HOME.
AND I'M NOT THERE. TO SAY NO.

TERESA I L--
CLK

TELL YOU ONE THING I'VE LEARNED, DIARY. ONE PITIFUL LITTLE LESSON TO DREDGE FROM THE HELL.

THE HUMAN BRAIN'S MORE MALLEABLE THAN WET-FUCKING-MUD.
OH, RESHAPE IT ALL YOU WANT. MOULD IT, BREAK IT, REFORM IT.
BUILD GLORIOUS CASTLES OR TOXIC SNAKES. DOESN'T MATTER.

THE SLIGHTEST PRESSURE AND IT'S MUSHED DOWN TO SLIME.

HA. TELL YOU WHAT. TELL YOU WHAT, DIARY-- LET'S *EXTEND* THAT NAFF LITTLE METAPHOR EVEN FURTHER, SHALL WE? NOTHING *BETTER* TO DO RIGHT NOW.

SO THIS *SMEAR*. THIS *STAIN* OF EXISTENTIAL HUMAN *PULP*. YOU WANT TO KNOW ALL ITS *GOOD* FOR, AFTER BEING RENDERED DOWN TO MUSH? I'LL TELL YOU:

CLINGING TO WHATEVER-THE-FUCK IT WAS SMEARED ON.
PFT. HOW'D YOU LIKE THAT-- 'S ALL *GONE*.
I'LL NIP DOWN THE SHOP.

YOU WANT ME TO C--
DON'T BE SILLY-- IT'S ONLY DOWNSTAIRS. JUST WATCH THE *KIDS*, EH?
ANYWAY.

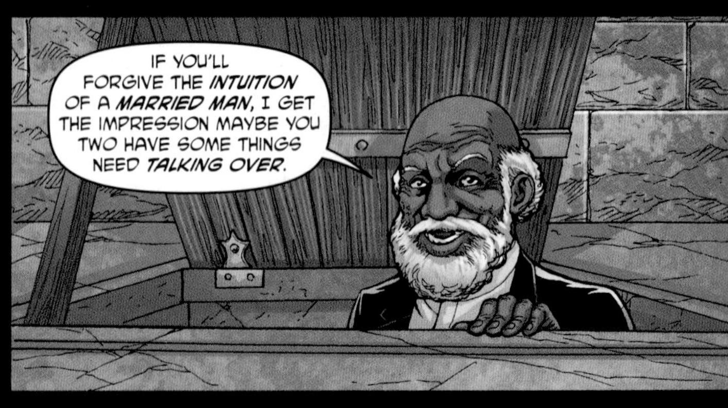

IF YOU'LL FORGIVE THE *INTUITION* OF A *MARRIED MAN*, I GET THE IMPRESSION MAYBE YOU TWO HAVE SOME THINGS NEED *TALKING OVER*.

WE DIDN'T KNOW.
WE DIDN'T KNOW.
OUR LAST *HOUR* TOGETHER.

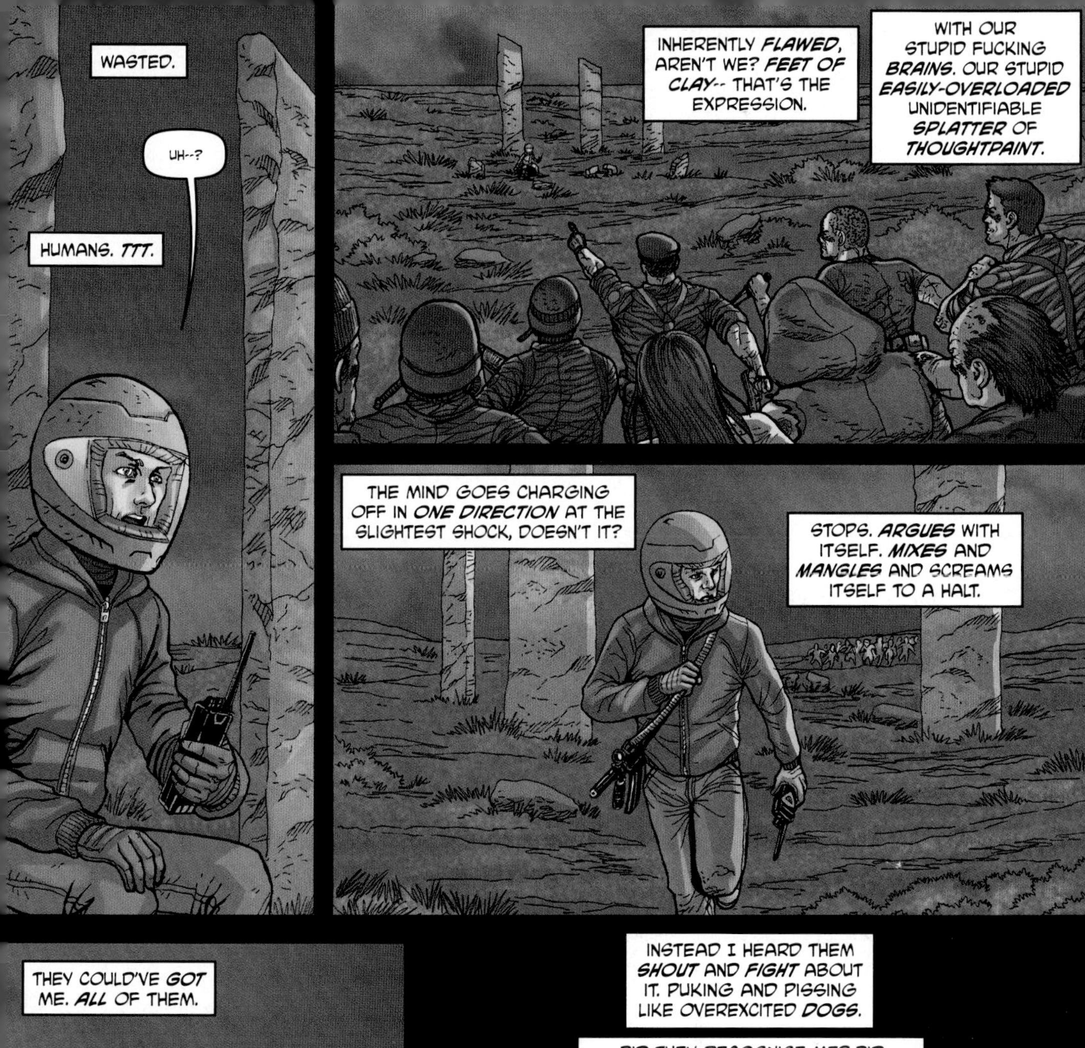

WASTED.
UH--?
HUMANS. TTT.
INHERENTLY FLAWED, AREN'T WE? FEET OF CLAY-- THAT'S THE EXPRESSION.
WITH OUR STUPID FUCKING BRAINS. OUR STUPID EASILY-OVERLOADED UNIDENTIFIABLE SPLATTER OF THOUGHTPAINT.
THE MIND GOES CHARGING OFF IN ONE DIRECTION AT THE SLIGHTEST SHOCK, DOESN'T IT?
STOPS. ARGUES WITH ITSELF. MIXES AND MANGLES AND SCREAMS ITSELF TO A HALT.

THEY COULD'VE GOT ME. ALL OF THEM.

ALL AT ONCE.

INSTEAD I HEARD THEM SHOUT AND FIGHT ABOUT IT. PUKING AND PISSING LIKE OVEREXCITED DOGS.

DID THEY RECOGNISE ME? DID THEY REMEMBER HER ORDERS? DID THEY BREAK THEIR BLOODY HEARTS CHOOSING BETWEEN THE CROSS AND THE CONTROL? FUCK KNOWS.

MYSTERIES, RIGHT? SAVE THEM FOR A WORLD WITH TIME TO THINK.

POINT IS, POINT IS: JUST THE ONE. JUST ONE RAGGED-BREATHED RUNNER FELL-IN BEHIND ME.

I THOUGHT: MAYBE I CAN OUTRUN JUST ONE.

HUMANS.
IT'S NOT THAT WE'VE GOT FEET OF CLAY, DIARY. IT'S THAT WE'VE GOT SHIT FOR BRAINS.

EVEN AT OUR *FINEST*. AT OUR MOST *CLEAR* AND *CERTAIN*.
EVEN WHEN THE MIND'S BEEN *FILED FREE* OF ALL THE JOINS, WHEN IT'S LEFT *PURE* AND *PERFECT*, WHEN IT'S A THING OF *AIM* AND *REWARD* WITHOUT THE SLIGHTEST *CRUMB* OF *COMPLEXITY* TO GET IN THE WAY--
--*STILL*.
STILL IT'S *DEFORMABLE*.
Y.
YOU KNOW WHAT SHE *SAID*. YOU'RE NOT SUPPOSED TO *HURT* ME.

...KK...
...HUKK...*HAHA*
LLLLEAVEHIMAAAAAAAAAGET GET LEAVE MAKEHERCOMMMME No No No HAHAH
RESHAPABLE. *TWISTABLE*.
CORRUPTIBLE.

THEY *OKAY?*
YEAHYEAH, PLAYING ON THE *STAIRS*.
SHOULDN'T WE KEEP THEM *UP* H--
THEY'RE *FINE*. MO LOCKS THE *FRONT* ON THE WAY OUT EVER SINCE *MOIRA* GOT OUT.
THEY'RE *FINE*.
CHEERS.
BRAINS.
WHAT A *MESS*, DIARY. WHAT A FUCKING MESS.
LISTEN, T--
NO, PLEASE, YOU G--
SHAKY, I--
REALLY, AFTER Y--
SORRY.
HA.
LIKE I SAID.
RESHAPABLE. *TWISTABLE*.
BRAAP
OH *SORRY*, *SORRY*, HA.
HA.
CORRUPTIBLE.

HERE'S THE *SECRET:* YOU CAN *USE* THAT. THE KNOWLEDGE OF THAT *FLAW*. THAT *MESS*.
TO NUDGE, TO STEER, TO *MANIPULATE*. TO CHANGE THE *GOALS*.
TO CORRUPT.

AND IT *IS* CORRUPTION, ISN'T IT? OH FUCK YES, IN THIS WORLD? OF *COURSE* IT IS. WE *CORRUPT* AND WE *INFECT* UNTIL ALL THAT REALLY MATTERS IS SMEARED-OVER SELFISH, SICK, SNAKEY *BRAINSHIT.*

'COURSE, THE FUNNY PART IS: YOU CAN'T STOP THE SAME THING HAPPENING TO *YOU.* THE WAY YOU THINK. THE WAY YOU SEE THINGS-- CHANGED FOREVER.

LIKE THE URGE TO ENDLESSLY ASK *WHY*. LIKE PRETENDING *LOVE'S* STILL A *THING*.
LIKE MAKING EXCUSES FOR *INTOXICATING* A *BEAUTIFUL MIND.*

LIKE SITTING HERE FOR *HOURS* WRITING-UP A DAY'S WORTH OF MIND-CRUSHINGLY *HORRIBLE EVENTS* IN A DIARY NOBODY'LL EVER READ.
POINTLESS.
AND ALL THE *REAL* STUFF? HA. ALL THE *IMPORTANT* STUFF?

THAT GETS *MISSED* IN THE *RUSH*.
...WWWAIT.
...

WHERE THE FUCK *IS* EVERYONE?

ENTRY #48. LET'S START WITH THE MOST OBVIOUS *UNDERSTATEMENT* OF *ALL TIME*. READY?

THE END OF THE WORLD IS A LONELY PLACE.
THEY LEFT.
I CHECKED THE WHOLE ISLAND. NO SIGN. NO SOUND. NO SOUND FOREVER.

I HAD A LITTLE CRY, DIARY. NOT SURE WHY. OVERLOAD. SOME BOLLOCKS LIKE THAT. I DON'T THINK YOU'D CALL IT MISERY. I THINK WE'RE PAST ANYTHING THAT RECOGNISABLE NOW.
THEY LEFT. THEY LEFT WHILE I WAS GONE AND I SUPPOSE THEY MUST'VE BANKED ON THE PLUSSIES WATCHING ME INSTEAD OF THEM.
I SUPPOSE THEY WERE RIGHT TOO.
HA.
HAHAHA.
JUST LIKE THAT. THOSE CLEVER, CLEVER LITTLE BASTARDS.

HAHAH--
HUH.
EXCEPT THAT THE BRAINDEAD IDIOTS CAME BACK AT DAWN, LIKE GHOSTS IN THE LIGHT.

JESUS FUCK WOULD YOU JUST LOOK AT THAT. "LIKE GHOSTS IN THE LIGHT." SOME BLOODY WRITER YOU ARE, SHAKY.
THE END OF THE WORLD MAY INDEED BE LONELY, BUT IT'S NOT HALF BLOODY PRETENTIOUS ABOUT IT.
'M.
'M A BIT DRUNK.
'SNOTHING WRONG WITHAT.
SO FUCK GHOSTS. FUCK WORDS. AND FUCK THE PRETENTION-- NONE OF IT'S WORTH THE PAPER IT'S SCRIBBLED ON.

MY WORLD CAME BACK WITH THE DAWN AND THE ONLY THING THAT MATTERS ABOUT THAT, DIARY, IS THE PROMISE THAT CAME WITH IT.
THE ONLY PROMISE THAT COUNTS, HERE IN WORLD 2.0:

"THIS ISN'T THE END, SHAKY. NOT YET."

"YOU'RE NOT ALONE."
"YOU'RE NOT ALONE."

WELL FUCK THAT FILTHY LYING PROMISE RIGHT IN ITS MAGGOTY FACE.
WHERE ... WHERE DID YOU GUYS GO...?
HEY, GUYS?
YOU DON'T HAVE TO BE ALONE TO BE LONELY.
SO, UH. L-LANCE?
LOOK... THESE BARRELS, MATE. YOU'VE ALL BEEN OFF ON FLOTTA, RIGHT? IT'S OIL. YOU'VE BEEN COLLECTING OIL.
IT'S FOR THE BIG ESC--
LANCE, DON'T Y...
HHH.
SON?
C'MON MATE. WE ALL AGREED.
BUT.
YOU'RE NOT ALONE, SHAKY. YOU'RE NOT ALONE.

YOU'RE NOT *ALONE.*
I WILL REMEMBER THAT KISS FOREVER.

SAVAGE.
THAT'S THE WORD.
LIKE... LIKE ONE SPLASH OF *SINGLE MALT* WAS ALL IT TOOK TO BURST A *BLOODY GREAT DAM.*
MORE EVEN THAN THE *LAST* TIME. IN THE *WOODS.* AFTER THE *FIT.*
THIS...
THIS WAS LIKE *OVERCOMPENSATING.* LIKE *PAYBACK* FOR A LIFE *WITHOUT INDULGENCE.*
LIKE...

LIKE REVENGE.
SMOKE.
BURNING ALL THE REST, AREN'T THEY?
OOOH, THEY'RE IN A RIGHT OLD MOOD.
YOU CAME IN, NICKED A BUNCH OF OIL. DID THEY LEAVE A SENTRY OR TWO, RAB? DID YOU KILL ANY OF 'EM?
I BET YOU DID.
YOU'RE PLAYING WITH FIRE, MATE.
"YOU NEED ME." THAT WAS THE LAME SUBTEXT, DIARY. THE PART I COULDN'T SAY.
"YOU'RE NOT AS CLEVER AS ME. NOT AS SNEAKY. YOU'LL ALWAYS NEED A WELL-OILED WEASEL. ONE CHIEFTAIN, ONE LEADER. SAME AS EVER."
LOOK. YOU NICK A FEW BARRELS. FINE. BUT EVEN IF THE BLOODY REFINERY'S STILL WORKING ON THAT THING IT WON'T GET YOU FAR.
YOU HAVEN'T THOUGHT THROUGH THIS BIG ESCAPE OF Y--
SHAKESPEARE.
"YOU NEED ME."
DON'T YOU TALK T'MY PEOPLE.
EVER AGAIN.

"PLEASE NEED ME."

T.
TERESA, I--
DON'T TALK.

WHATEVER ELSE, SHAKY.
DON'T TALK.

SO ALL HAIL CHIEF *RAB*, I SUPPOSE.

CLEVER OLD SHIT HAD THE *CRUDE* STASHED-AWAY IN THE *REFINERY-SHIP* LONG BEFORE *THEY* CAME *SNIFFING*.

MY GUESS? HE'S LOOKING TO COOK-UP SOME *DIESEL*. *JUST* ENOUGH TO HAUL-OUT ON ONE OF THE *BIG BOATS*.

NOT THAT MY GUESS COUNTS FOR *MUCH* NOW. AND IF THE REFINERY'S ACTUALLY *WORKING I* CAN'T BLOODY HEAR IT. SO... SO WHEN THE PLUSSIES *DID* COME...
(...BUZZING ROUND LIKE ANGRY WASPS... SHOUTING AT EACH OTHER AS MUCH AS US...)
...WHEN THEY *DID* COME RAB'S PEOPLE STOOD AND *SHRUGGED*. LIKE *BUTTER WOULDN'T MELT*. LIKE *INNOCENT SCHOOLKIDS* GETTING THE *EYE* FROM AN ANGRY *TEACHER*.
LIKE: "PLEASE, SIR-- IT WASN'T ME, SIR."

S-SINCE WHEN DID THE *CROSSED* NEED A FUCKING *EXCUSE* TO HAND OUT *DETENTIONS?*

SINCE THE *HEADMISTRESS* SAID SO, DIARY. SINCE *SHE* GOT THEM SO *TURNED ROUND* IN THEIR OWN *BRAINS* THEY DON'T KNOW WHAT'S *INSTINCT* AND WHAT'S *INDOCTRINATION* ANY MORE.

I TRIED *SWITCHING-ON* THE RADIO THREE TIMES.

NOT A *SOUND*.

NOT A *SIGHT*, EITHER. NOT OF HER.
SO THEY CIRCLED AND BARKED AND HOWLED LIKE *RABID DOGS*--

--WITH JUST ENOUGH *BRAINS* LEFT TO REMEMBER THE *"SSSSSIIIIT"* COMMAND THEY'D BEEN *GIVEN*--

--AND SLOWLY TESTED THE BOUNDS OF THEIR *FREEDOM*.

THEY WENT YAPPING OFF AFTER THAT.
BACK TO THE HILLS. BACK TO WATCHING. BACK TO WAITING.
MAYBE THEY WERE... SATISFIED AT THE TOLL THEY'D TAKEN. ONE LIFE FOR A FEW BARRELS. PAYBACK.
MAYBE JUST GUILTY ABOUT ACTING WITHOUT PERMISSION.
FUCKSAKES. LOOK AT THAT. LOOK! THOSE WORDS DON'T MAKE SENSE. "WAITING." "SATISFIED." "GUILTY." NOT CROSSED WORDS. NOT LIFE 2.0 WORDS.
IT WOULD'VE BEEN REMARKABLE ONCE TO WATCH THEM TURNING AWAY INSTEAD OF SPRINTING AT US.
NOT NOW. NONE OF IT MATTERS NOW.
NOT IN THE END OF TIMES.
WE'RE JUST FIDDLING, DIARY, WHILE ROME BURNS. JUST WAITING FOR FATE.
AND SO ARE THE CROSSED.
SHAKY...?

A WORD.
IS. IS THE REFINERY WORKING? I CAN'T HEAR I--
AYE-- IT'S WORKIN' JUST FINE.
I THOUGHT...
I THOUGHT MAYBE Y'DESERVE T'HEAR A SPOT AY TRUTH BEFORE WE SET OOT. AN EXPLANATION T'TAKE WI' YOU ON YER JOURNEY. SO.
YOU ARE A CRAWLING MANIPULATIVE SNAKE WI'OOT A SPOT AY TRUST FOR ANYONE.
STANDS T'REASON OTHER FOLKS COULDNAE TRUST YOU NOW IF THEY TRIED.
WH--
OCH-- IT'S NOT THAT YOU'RE SELFISH, EXACTLY... IT'S MORE THAT YOU'LL ALWAYS ACT FROM THE POINT AY VIEW OF THE SELF-- Y'KNOW? IT'S DIFFERENT.
YOU CANNAE SHARE. YOU CANNAE EMPATHISE. YOU CANNAE EVEN CONCEIVE OF A WORLD THAT WOULDNAE BENEFIT FROM HAVING YOU IN IT.
HHH.
YOU'VE SAID BEFORE NOW YOU'VE ONLY TH'BEST INTERESTS AY THE ISLAND AT HEART, AND IT COULD BE Y'RIGHT ABOOT THAT. I HOPE SO, LAD.
I HOPE SO, BECAUSE IT'LL HELP YE UNDERSTAND WHAT'S ABOUT T'HAPPEN.
SHAKESPEARE, HERE IS THE VERY SIMPLE TRUTH:

FOLKS AROUND YOU DIE A WEE BIT TOO MUCH.
T.
TERESA.
SHH.

WE'RE LEAVING THIS PLACE, LADDIE.
EVERYTHING'S SET.

...I LOVE YOU.

WE'RE LEAVING AND YOU'RE NOT COMING.

WHAT'RE Y--
NO--

OH GOD.
I.
I LOVE YOU TOO.

ENTRY #49. DUSK.
I CAN WRITE AT LEAST. VERY FUCKING NOBLE, THAT. THE EPISTOLIC CRIPPLE. THE ONE NARCISSISTIC URGE THAT DOESN'T DIE ALONG WITH LIFESAVING MOBILTY.
SO. SO.
AFTER A FEW HOURS THE PAIN BECAME BEARABLE.
THE QUIET WILL NOT.

THEY'RE LEAVING. THEY SMEARED THEIR BOATS WITH PITCH AND THEY'RE SLINKING INTO THE NIGHT.
THE JOURNEY'S OVER. FOR ME. FOR ME.
DEAD SOON.
AND ALL THEY SAID, DIARY, WAS:
"YOU'RE NOT COMING."

THERE'S A SICK JOKE IN THAT.

I DON'T KNOW. I DON'T KNOW WHAT WAS HAPPENING THAT DAY.
SEEMS... CRUDE, DOESN'T IT? --NO, WORSE, IT SEEMS DISAPPOINTING-- THAT MY HAIRY BRITISH CODGERS SHOULD PLAY A CENTRAL ROLE IN THE GHASTLY CLUSTERFUCK THAT IS MY PRESENT LIFE. BUT FITTING. FITTING THAT IT COMES DOWN TO SEX.
YOU MISTAKE ME FOR A MAN OF DEPTH AT YOUR PERIL.
MY BRAIN. MY BALLS. NEITHER WERE IN ANY HURRY THAT DAY.
IT'D BEEN MONTHS. THE ONE TIME WE'D COME CLOSE BEFORE-- ME AND HER? WELL. YOU KNOW WHAT HAPPENED THERE.
NOT MUCH CHANCE OF A CHEEKY TUG ON THE ROAD SINCE. BY ALL RIGHTS I SHOULD'VE BEEN MR BLUE-BOLLOCKS McSPEEDYSQUIRT, BUT IT WASN'T ME RUSHING AHEAD THAT DAY. WASN'T ME HITTING CRITICAL MASS.
WASN'T ME TRYING TO HOLD-OFF.
N-NNNNO. OH.
NO NO NO OH MY LORD, OH MY GOD--

OH. OH NO.
BUT THEN... THAT'S HER ALL OVER, ISN'T IT? THAT'S HER MAGIC.

ALL ALONG YOU THINK SHE'S FIERCE, INDOMITABLE, STEELY EYED.
NNNNN

ALL ALONG YOU THINK SHE'S IN CHARGE.
TH.
THEY'RE WAITING. THEY KNOW.

BUT SHE'S NOT. NOT REALLY.
NO OH
NO
OH GGGG
ALL SHE DOES.
ALL SHE'S GOOD AT.
ALL SHE'S EVER BEEN GOOD AT--
IS THIS:

HOLDING BACK PASSION.

AND EVEN THEN, NEVER FOR LONG.
UUUUUUUUUUHHHHHHHHHH

I'VE.
I'VE NEVER.
THAT'S.
THAT'S THE FIRST TIME I'VE BEEN ABLE TO...
SHAKY, D-DID YOU.
YOU KNOW.
DID YOU. *YET*.

DIARY: YOU CAN *KEEP* YOUR *STORY NEATNESS*. YOU CAN KEEP YOUR *SYMMETRY* AND YOUR *CLEVER FUCKING BOOKENDS*. YOU CAN KEEP YOUR *STARCROSSED DRAMA* AND *PROFOUND THEMES*.

HERE-- YOU *UNBELIEVABLE BASTARDS* OF *HEREAFTER*-- HERE IS THE *FEEBLE* SECRET THAT UNDERPINS THE *WRETCHED, LAUGHABLE MYSTERY* THAT IS ME.

UH.
N.
NEARLY THERE.

AT THE *END OF THE WORLD* I MADE *LOVE* TO THE WOMAN I *ADORED*.

AND I *COULDN'T COME*.

ENTRY-THE-LAST.
I SIT. I WAIT. AND I REALISE-- JUST A SMIDGEON FUCKING LATE, ACTUALLY-- THAT THAT'S BASICALLY HOW IT'S BEEN FROM THE START.
FUNNY, ISN'T IT? EVEN AFTER EVERYTHING I'M STILL STUPID.
LIKE... LIKE HOURS BEFORE DAWN ON THE LAST DAY, I... OH FUCK. HA. I HONESTLY THOUGHT WE WERE DONE WITH WORDS. IDIOT.
NO MORE TALKING. NO MORE SMART-MONKEY PRETENCE AT COMMUNICATION. THE POT'D BUBBLED OVER. THE CASCADE WAS UNDERWAY.

I THINK BACK, I THINK BACK (WHAT THE PISS'VE I GOT LEFT?) AND WHAT'S THERE IS ONE OF THE FIRST LESSONS I LEARNT.
"DAYDREAMERS NEVER LAST."
BUT WHEN THERE'S NO FUCKING WORDS AND NO FUCKING ANSWERS IT TURNS OUT SUPPOSITION-- BLOODY IMAGINATION-- THAT'S ALL YOU'VE GOT.

LIKE... HAVE A THINK ABOUT RAB'S PLANS, DIARY. HIM AND ALL MY PEOPLE. THE PLANS THEY WOULDN'T SHARE. THE PLANS THEY HID.
(THEY'RE ALL GONE NOW.)
I SAT THERE ABOVE THE BEACH AND I IMAGINED WHAT THE FUCK THEY'D BEEN MEANING TO DO WITH THEIR... THEIR BIG OLD REFINERY SHIP. THEIR STOLEN PITTANCE OF CRUDE OIL.
HAD THEY MEANT TO... OUTRUN THE CROSSED? WAS THAT IT? TO OUTSHOOT THEM? TO RUN THE BLOCKADE WHILE THE PLUSSIES WERE BUSY SWOOPING-DOWN ON ME?
BRAVE. DESPERATE. CRAZY. STUPID. THAT'S WHAT I WAS THINKING.
A STUPID PLAN EVEN BEFORE WE KNEW HOW MANY OF THE CROSS-FACED CUNTS THERE REALLY WERE.

BUT THEN... HUH. HERE'S THE THING WITH *SUPPOSITION*. YOU GET *GOING* AND YOU CAN'T *STOP.*

NOT JUST THE *COULDA WOULDA SHOULDAS* EITHER, BUT THE BEHIND-THE-SCENES BOLLOCKS YOU NEVER BOTHERED THINKING *THROUGH* AT THE TIME.

THE *MYSTERIES* YOU'VE BEEN TRYING TO *IGNORE*.

FOR INSTANCE:

OLD MO? HE'D DONE THE *BOOZE RUN* A DOZEN TIMES SINCE WE HOLED-UP WITH HIM.
NIP DOWN THE LOCAL *SHOP--* JUST ROUND THE CORNER. SUPPLIES, WATER, FRESH BOTTLE OF THE *HIGHLANDS' BEST.*
FLOWER OF SCOTLAND
DID HE HEAR THEM ON HIS WAY *BACK?* DISTANT *LAUGHTER*... FAINT *SHOUTING*...?
I SUPPOSE HE *MUST'VE*. I REMEMBER HE SAID "THEY'RE OUT THERE"-- JUST BEFORE THE *END*.
WHEN I HAD *OTHER THINGS* ON MY MIND.

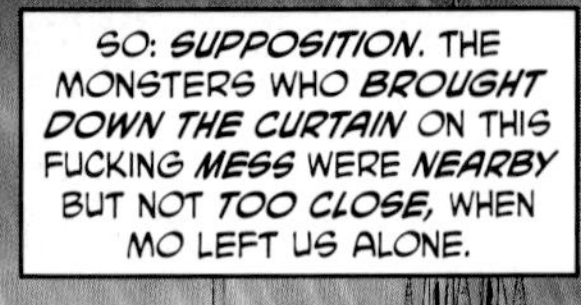

SO: *SUPPOSITION*. THE MONSTERS WHO *BROUGHT DOWN THE CURTAIN* ON THIS FUCKING *MESS* WERE *NEARBY* BUT NOT *TOO CLOSE,* WHEN MO LEFT US ALONE.

THE TIMING'S *WRONG* FOR THAT. THEY WOULD'VE PINPOINTED US *SOONER* IF THEY'D BEEN *RIGHT THERE OUTSIDE* FROM THE *START*.

HEAR? HEAR?
WHERE WHERE WHERE
BE NICE TO *MYTHOLOGISE*, WOULDN'T IT? FOR THE SAKE OF TIDINESS.
LIKE, THEY WERE *PEOPLE* WE'D MET ALONG THE WAY. SIGNIFICANT *PLAYERS* FROM OUR *ADVENTURE* COMING-BACK LIKE *BAD PENNIES*. LIKE *BOOKENDS*.
THEY *WEREN'T*. LIFE 2.0 DOESN'T *WORK* LIKE THAT.

WHICH, OF COURSE, IS SOMETHING YOU'VE GOT TO BUILD INTO YOUR PRESENT-DAY SUPPOSITIONS TOO, OH DOOMED LITTLE DAYDREAMER.
NOTHING'S *TIDY.* NOTHING'S *SURE.* THE STORY GETS *JUMBLED* AND THE *SUPPOSITIONS* WON'T *FLOAT.*
LIKE... LIKE LET'S SUPPOSE SHE CAME TO CAVA BECAUSE OF ME. (TO WHATEVER FUCKING END.)
LET'S SUPPOSE SHE'S BEEN *HOLDING BACK* HER *PACK* ALL THIS TIME.
LET'S SUPPOSE *"CONTROL"* IS HER *THING.*
SEEMS FAIR, DOESN'T IT? CONTROL'S HER *THING* AND THAT'S *LUCKY*, BECAUSE SHE'S *ALL THAT STANDS BETWEEN US AND THEM.*
BUT THEN YOU RUN OUT OF SUPPOSITIONS AND YOU CRASH INTO THE *EVIDENCE*. YOU SEE THE *LOOKS* HER MONSTERS *SHOOT HER*. THE *CRINGES* SIDE-BY-SIDE WITH *BITTER SCOWLS*. THE *FEAR/HATE*.

AND SO, THANKS TO THAT ONE, WEAK, RANK LITTLE *CHAIN OF DAYDREAMS* YOU'RE OBLIGATED TO *ACCEPT*-- LIKE *ALL OF US* LAST NIGHT--
--THAT SHE'S NOT AS *IN CONTROL* AS WE THOUGHT.
LEAVE TH'REST. JUST GET READY.

SHE WAS *THERE* WHEN THE GAMEKEEPER CALLED ME, RIGHT? SO WAS THAT TO MAKE SURE HE PASSED ON SOME... SOME OBLIQUE *MESSAGE* I WAS TOO STUPID TO HEAR?
...OR JUST BECAUSE SHE COULDN'T LEAVE HIM *ALONE* ANY MORE? DIDN'T HAVE ANYONE ELSE TO *DEFEND* HIM?
AFTER ALL-- IT WASN'T LONG AFTER THAT THE PRIEST CAME AND GOT *UPPITY* ALL ON HIS OWN, REMEMBER? SHOT *MARIA*. TESTING HIS *BOUNDS*.

AND ALL BECAUSE *SHE* COULDN'T KEEP AN EYE ON *BOTH* HER *PET MONSTERS* AT ONCE.
SSSSHAKESSSSPEEEEEAAAARE
I WAS WRONG TO THINK SHE WAS *IN CONTROL*.
JUST LIKE I WAS *WRONG* TO THINK WE'D RUN OUT OF *WORDS*.

WORDS ARE ALL ANY OF US HAVE LEFT.
WHERE!? WHERE!?

Y'KNOW... EVEN THEN WE COULD'VE GOT AWAY WITH IT.
MO KNEW HIS TOWN. KNEW HIS ROUTE.

EVEN THEN IT ALL COULD'VE ENDED SO DIFFERENTLY.
IF ONLY THERE'D BEEN NO MORE WORDS.

QUESTIONS.
WH... WH...
TIME TO ASK QUESTIONS.

I FOUGHT FOR CALM DIARY. THAT OLD MENTAL MUSCLE.
I FOUGHT FOR CONTROL.

R-RIGHT. RIGHT, YEAH.
I DO HAVE QU--
ME FIRST.

...
THERE?
YOU THERE?
Y... YES, I. S-SORRY.
SORRY.
IT... IT JUST HADN'T OCCURRED TO ME YOU'D HAVE QUESTIONS TOO.
THE CHURCH.
YOU REMEMBER THE CHURCH?
I'M... I'M ALMOST THERE.
YES.
YES, OF COURSE. GOD. THERE'S NOT A DAY PASSES I DON'T WISH I'D D--
No.
NOT THAT CHURCH.
THE OTHER CHURCH.

DIARY. DIARY, IT WAS AT ABOUT THAT POINT.
THE MARY CHURCH.
THAT I BEGAN TO CRAWL.
WE'RE GOING TO HAVE TO FIGHT.
NO NO NO NO NO
WE SHOT. BOOM. BOOM. WE FOUGHT.
NEED TO KNOW NEED TO KNOW.
AND OHHH, DIARY, YOU COULD HEAR IT AND SEE IT AND FEEL IT.

(HER TREMBLING. HER SHAKING AND FALLING APART.

HER, FRAGILE. HER SOBBING AND YES OH-SO-FUCKING FRAGILE RIGHT THERE IN FRONT OF HER EVIL HORDE.)

SHE WAS THE ONLY THING BETWEEN US AND THEM.

AND IT TURNED OUT SHE WAS MADE OF PAPER ALL ALONG.

DID SHE *HIT* ANY PLUSSIES THAT DAY? FUCK KNOWS. *FUCK* KNOWS.

SUCH A *LITTLE THING*. SUCH A LITTLE THING TO BE *SO IMPORTANT*. (OR... OR SUCH A *BIG THING* FOR ME TO'VE MISTAKEN AS *TRIVIAL*...?)

HE SAID --YOU REMEMBER?-- HE SAID HE THOUGHT SHE'D NEVER KILLED ANYONE.
HE SAID THE *OTHERS* RESPECTED THAT IN HER. HE SAID THEY UNDERSTOOD THAT MEANT SHE WAS *STRONG*.

MAKE HER *STRONG*, I THOUGHT.
MAKE HER *STRONG*.

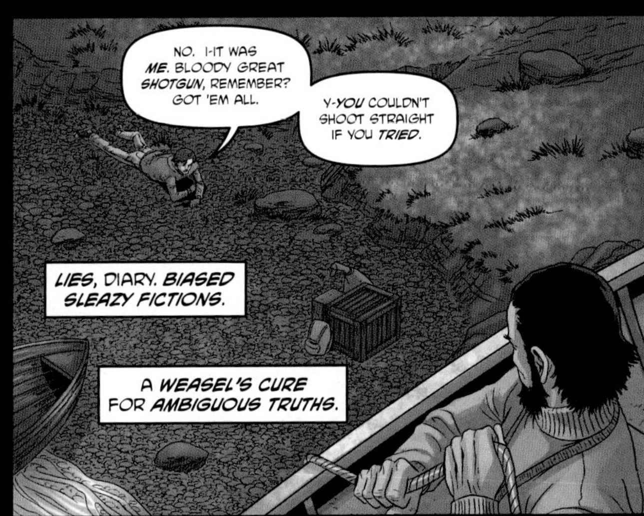
NO. I-IT WAS *ME*. BLOODY GREAT *SHOTGUN*, REMEMBER? GOT 'EM ALL.
Y-*YOU* COULDN'T SHOOT STRAIGHT IF YOU *TRIED*.
LIES, DIARY. *BIASED SLEAZY FICTIONS*.
A *WEASEL'S CURE* FOR *AMBIGUOUS TRUTHS*.

(SEE ALSO:)
I'M *CLOSE*, OHGOD, I'M *RRRREALLY* CLOSE.

I WASN'T.

TH. THANK YOU.
THANK YOU.
YOUR TURN. QUESTION QUESTION.

WAIT... DO... DO YOU HEAR SOMETHING..?

QUESTIONS. QUESTIONS. MY HEAD WAS FUCKED. TOO MANY TO PICK FROM.
I DON'T MIND TELLING YOU, DIARY. AS I CRAWLED (KNOWING THE WHERE BUT NOT THINKING). AS I CRAWLED THERE I DID A LITTLE PISS IN MY PANTS. LIKE-- OVERWHELMED. CRITICAL-HA-HA-HA-MASS.
AND YOU KNOW, YOU KNOW WHAT? EVEN WITH EVERYTHING ELSE RAGING ROUND IT I REMEMBER FEELING ASHAMED ABOUT THAT.
THAT'S EVERYTHING YOU EVER NEEDED TO KNOW ABOUT THE HUMAN BRAIN.

WHY DID YOU M... MAKE ME TALK TO HIM.
THE GAMEKEEPER?

SSSHH. I-IT'S THE KIDS CHEERING.
MEANS. MEANS MO'S BACK, SHAKY. MO'S COMING.
I. I DON'T WANT HIM TO SEE US LIKE TH--
WAIT. H-HANG ON.

TRAP.
ENVELOPE TRAP.
T-TURN YOU. TURN YOU GIVE CROSS BUT SAFE. NO DAMAGE NO RISK.

BUT--
DIDN'T WORK. SO. S-SO MADE YOU TALK TO HIM INSTEAD.
NEED. NEEDED YOU TO SEE WHAT HE IS.
HANG ON. W-WAIT.
SHAKY, WE HAVE TO ST--
JUST WAIT!
NEEDED YOU TO SEE HIM AS NNNNNOTHING.
WH... WHY W--
BECAUSE I CAN'T.
YOU WANT TO KNOW WHAT I WAS THINKING, DIARY? CRUEL, UNSYMPATHETIC DRIBBLE OF SHIT THAT I AM?
I WAS THINKING: OH. OH, MY LOVE...
YOU USED TO BE SO STRONG.
B-BUT WHY DID Y--
NO. MY TURN. QUESTIONQUESTIONQUESTION.

GET OFF GET OFF SH--

DO YOU LOVE ME?

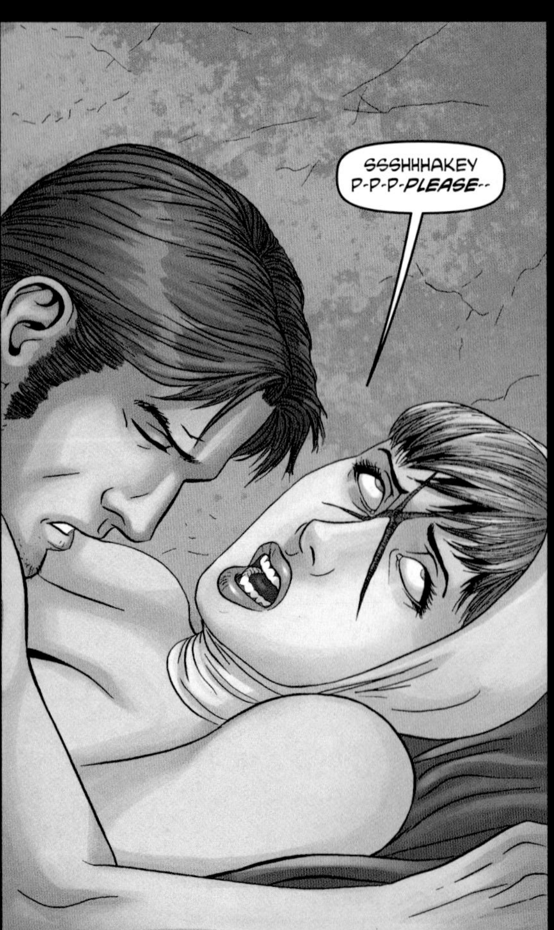
SSSHHHAKEY P-P-P-PLEASE--

...
...
...
YES.

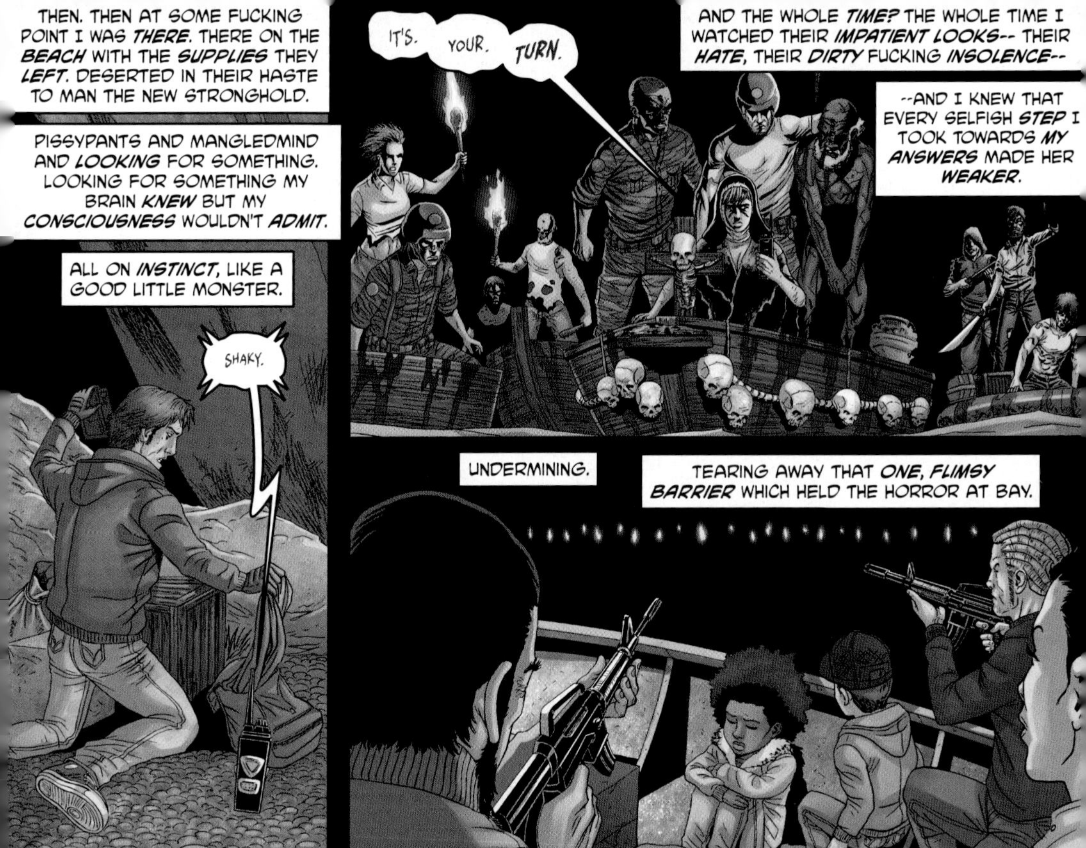
THEN. THEN AT SOME FUCKING POINT I WAS *THERE*. THERE ON THE *BEACH* WITH THE *SUPPLIES* THEY *LEFT*. DESERTED IN THEIR HASTE TO MAN THE NEW STRONGHOLD.
PISSYPANTS AND MANGLEDMIND AND *LOOKING* FOR SOMETHING. LOOKING FOR SOMETHING MY BRAIN *KNEW* BUT MY *CONSCIOUSNESS* WOULDN'T *ADMIT*.
ALL ON *INSTINCT*, LIKE A GOOD LITTLE MONSTER.
SHAKY.
IT'S.
YOUR.
TURN.
AND THE WHOLE *TIME?* THE WHOLE TIME I WATCHED THEIR *IMPATIENT LOOKS*-- THEIR *HATE*, THEIR *DIRTY* FUCKING *INSOLENCE*--
--AND I KNEW THAT EVERY SELFISH *STEP* I TOOK TOWARDS *MY ANSWERS* MADE HER *WEAKER*.
UNDERMINING.
TEARING AWAY THAT *ONE, FLIMSY BARRIER* WHICH HELD THE HORROR AT BAY.

SO I THOUGHT, *HEY*. CUT TO THE FUCKING *POINT*.
AOILEANN...

NK

WHAT DO YOU *WANT*, AOILEANN?
WHAT DO YOU *REALLY* WANT?

D... DON'T YOU KNOW?
HOW DON'T YOU KNNNNOOOOW?
OH
I WANT.
FOR US.
TO SAVE.
EACH OTHER.
OH GOD.

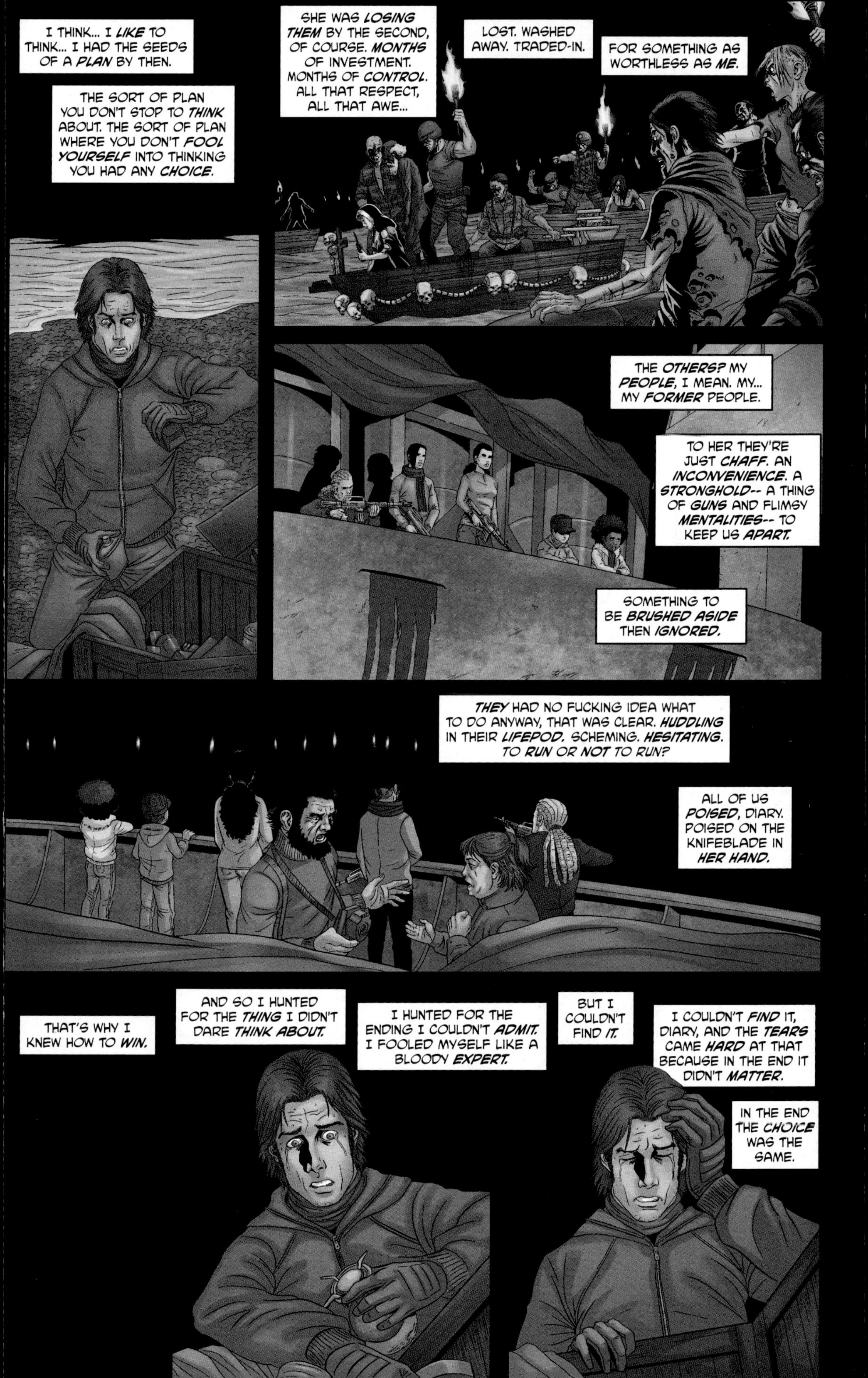
I THINK... I LIKE TO THINK... I HAD THE SEEDS OF A PLAN BY THEN.
THE SORT OF PLAN YOU DON'T STOP TO THINK ABOUT. THE SORT OF PLAN WHERE YOU DON'T FOOL YOURSELF INTO THINKING YOU HAD ANY CHOICE.
SHE WAS LOSING THEM BY THE SECOND, OF COURSE. MONTHS OF INVESTMENT. MONTHS OF CONTROL. ALL THAT RESPECT, ALL THAT AWE...
LOST. WASHED AWAY. TRADED-IN.
FOR SOMETHING AS WORTHLESS AS ME.
THE OTHERS? MY PEOPLE, I MEAN. MY... MY FORMER PEOPLE.
TO HER THEY'RE JUST CHAFF. AN INCONVENIENCE. A STRONGHOLD-- A THING OF GUNS AND FLIMSY MENTALITIES-- TO KEEP US APART.
SOMETHING TO BE BRUSHED ASIDE THEN IGNORED.
THEY HAD NO FUCKING IDEA WHAT TO DO ANYWAY, THAT WAS CLEAR. HUDDLING IN THEIR LIFEPOD. SCHEMING. HESITATING. TO RUN OR NOT TO RUN?
ALL OF US POISED, DIARY. POISED ON THE KNIFEBLADE IN HER HAND.
THAT'S WHY I KNEW HOW TO WIN.
AND SO I HUNTED FOR THE THING I DIDN'T DARE THINK ABOUT.
I HUNTED FOR THE ENDING I COULDN'T ADMIT. I FOOLED MYSELF LIKE A BLOODY EXPERT.
BUT I COULDN'T FIND IT.
I COULDN'T FIND IT, DIARY, AND THE TEARS CAME HARD AT THAT BECAUSE IN THE END IT DIDN'T MATTER.
IN THE END THE CHOICE WAS THE SAME.

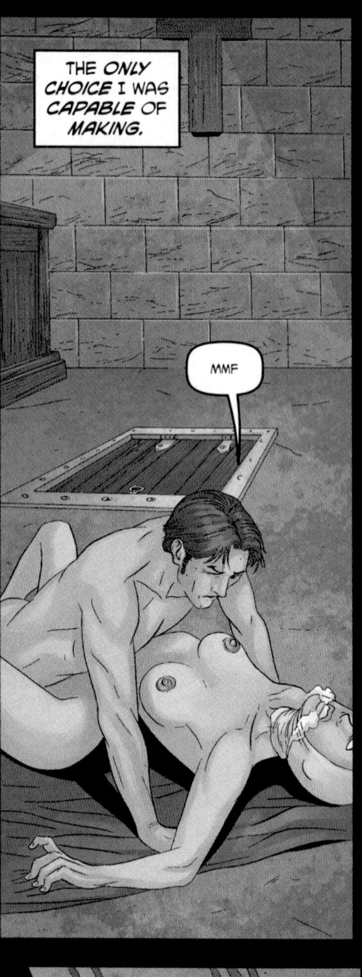
THE ONLY CHOICE I WAS CAPABLE OF MAKING.
MMF

M-M'LOVE.
MY LOVE, LISTEN.

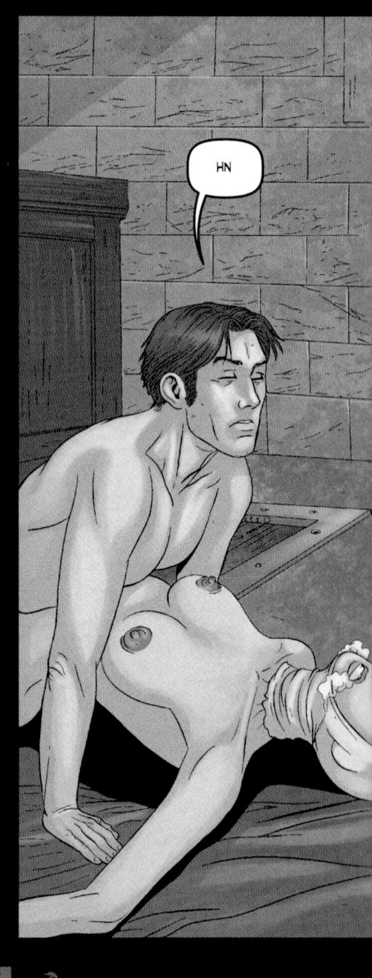
HN

YOU... YOU NEED TO BE STRONG. YOU NEED TO SHOW YOUR PEOPLE.
THEY'RE. THEY'RE WATCHING YOU. THEY'RE LISTENING.
YOU NEED TO FUCKING LEAD THEM, TERESA.

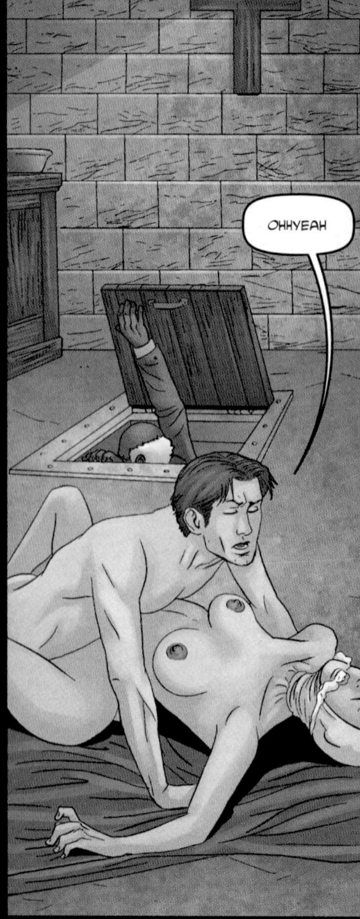
OHHYEAH

YOU NEED TO SHOW THEM YOU'RE NOT WEAK.

WHICH MEANS YOU NEED TO GIVE THEM *ME*.

SHAKY... THERE ARE S-SOME...
THEY'RE OUT THERE.
WH... WHAT ON *EARTH* ARE Y--

YOU GIVE THEM *ME*. YOU *SHOW THEM* YOU *CAN*. YOU... YOU SHOW THEM YOU CAN *DESTROY* WHAT YOU *LOVE*.
AND THE OTHERS. M-*MY* PEOPLE...
THE OTHERS LEAVE.

S-*STOP* IT!
FOR GOD'S *SAKE*, MAN! *STOP IT!* SHE'S HAVING A F--

DIARY, LISTEN:
No No
No No
I DIDN'T KNOW WHAT SHE WAS REALLY PLANNING, GATHERING THEM ALL TOGETHER LIKE THAT. STILL DON'T. I MEAN FUCK, MAYBE IT WAS NOTHING.
MAYBE IT WASN'T HER CHOICE AT ALL.
MAYBE THIS WHOLE TIME SHE'D... SHE'D BEEN MAKING ONE SPASTIC ATTEMPT TO HOLD THINGS TOGETHER AFTER ANOTHER.

WOULDN'T SURPRISE ME. NOTHING'S NEAT ANYMORE.
SHAKY!

BUT THE MORE SHE SOBBED THE MORE SHE LOST CONTROL. THE THINNER THE CAGE HOLDING HER PEOPLE FROM MINE.
AND I WOULD SAVE RAB AND THE REST. I'D FUCKING DECIDED THAT, DIARY.
I'D FUCKING SAVE THEM, THOSE CUNTS-- ME! --AND FOR THAT...?

FOR THAT ALL I NEEDED TO DO--
JUST A MMMINUTE--!
(SAME AS EVER. SAME AS EVER.)

--WAS TAKE THE DECISION OUT OF HER HANDS.

I *HOPE*... (I'M NOT TOO PROUD TO ADMIT IT). I HOPE THEY COULD SEE ME. MY PEOPLE. *MY* PEOPLE.

I HOPE THEY KNEW WHAT I WAS *DOING*. WHAT I WAS *TRYING* TO DO.

OPENING A WINDOW FOR THEM. STEALING THE HORROR FOR MYSELF. *DIVERTING* THE *HATE*.

THE BARREL OF BUTTER. OUR VERY OWN *SACRIFICIAL ALTAR*.

HUH. *FUCK IT.* NO POINT BEING *MYSTERIOUS* ANY MORE, I SUPPOSE. NOT NOW.

I WAS LOOKING FOR THE *CLAYMORE*, IF YOU MUST KNOW. BACK ON THE BEACH. THAT... THAT *PLAN* I DIDN'T WANT TO *DWELL ON*.

THE LAST *LANDMINE* FROM *INVERNESS*.

YES, FINE, NOT TOO *ORIGINAL*, AS FAR AS GLORIOUS HEROIC SCHEMES GO. DRAW THEM ONTO THE *ROCK*, BLOW THEM TO *HELL*, SAVE THE *DAY*.

BRUCE CUNTING-WILLIS.

BUT I COULDN'T *FIND* THE BASTARD BOMB, AND THINGS ARE NEVER THAT FUCKING *SIMPLE*, SO I DON'T SUPPOSE WE'LL GET THE CHANCE-- WILL WE DIARY, YOU AND ME? --TO FIND OUT IF THIS WEASELLY LITTLE *SHIT* HAS THE *BOLLOCKS* AFTER ALL.

TO DO IT TO HIMSELF.

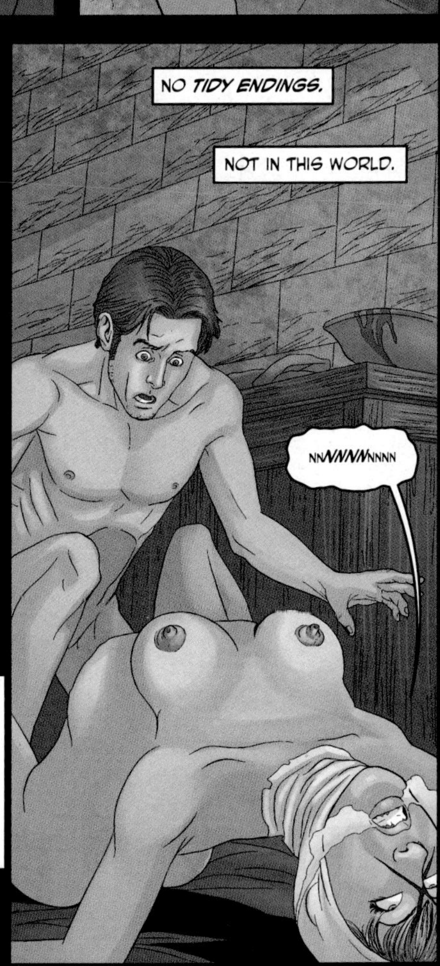

NNNNNNNNNAAAAAAA
BUT I'D GOT THEIR ATTENTION, THE PLUSFACED PRICKS. THAT'S WHAT MATTERED.
AND I GUESS I THOUGHT... I THOUGHT THAT AS LONG AS I COULD KEEP IT FOR JUST A LITTLE WHILE--

JUST.
JUST FOR A MINUTE.

--THEN THE OTHERS COULD GET AWAY.
S-START TH'ENGINE.

AND I DIDN'T SUPPOSE IT MATTERED MUCH WHAT HAPPENED TO ME.

MMF.

ALL RIGHT.
ALL RIGHT.
LET'S BE HAVING YOU.

PLEASE. PLEASE.
NOT LIKE THIS. NOT LIKE THIS.
I NEED YOU.
(FOR WHAT, DIARY? FOR FUCKING WHAT!?)
BOAT'S BUGGERED. TOO LATE.
S-SO YOU SET YOUR FACE.
YOU DON'T PLEAD.
YOU DON'T GIVE THEM THE SATISFACTION.
AND YOU SEND THEM OVER. I'M... I'M READY.
HRRR
I'M READY AND... AND I-IF YOU WANT THE TRUTH, LOVE...

...AND HERE, OH SHIMMERING JUDGEMENTAL NON-AUDIENCE, OH HATEFUL GODS OF EARTH 2.0, OH CLUSTERFUCKING SPIRITS OF HEROIC EXPECTATION--
HERE'S WHAT IT REALLY ALL CAME DOWN TO.
THIS SAVES ME.
GLORIOUS MARTYR SINS WASHED CLEAN SELFLESS WAY-OUT SAVE YOUR PEOPLE REMEMBERED FONDLY FOREVER WHEN IT CAME DOWN TO IT HE DID THE RIGHT THING.
R-REDEEMED.
VAIN, PREENING, SELFISH, LUCKY, LUCKY CUNT.
GOD I HATE YOU, SHAKESPEARE.

TOO EASY. TOO EASY LAZY EEEASY.
NOT FAIR. NOT HOW IT'S SUPPOSED TO G--
AOILEANN... P-PLEASE.
FOR ME.
AND IN THE END.
IN THE END SHE DID IT FOR LOVE.
HHHHHHHHE'S NOTHING.
HE'S NOTHING FLOPPYHAIR CUNT WWRRRRRRITER TAKE HIM--

AND THEY CAME.
GO. GO.
KILL RIP RAPE

AND THE OTHERS LEFT.
AND SHE SOBBED BETWEEN THE SNARLS AND
SHE. DID IT. FOR LOVE.
AND--

SUPERCROSSED. WE'VE. WE'VE ALL GIVEN THAT SOME THOUGHT, HAVEN'T WE? WE'VE DAYDREAMED AND CONJECTURED AND FAILED TO FUCKING IGNORE THAT SINGULAR MYSTERY.

A SMART MONSTER IN THE HILLS. A CAPTAIN OF DEMONS.

WE GUESSED WRONG, DIARY.

IT WAS *HIM*. FOR FUCK'S SAKE IT WAS *HIM*.

THE *BRIGHT ONE*. THE *CUNNING ONE*. THE *DEADLY ONE*. THE *PATIENT ONE*.

WAITING FOR THE *LIMELIGHT*. WAITING FOR THE *COURAGE* TO MOVE AGAINST HER. WAITING FOR HER TO *CRUMBLE* JUST ENOUGH--

--TO HAVE HIS *MOMENT*.
OHHHHHHHHH
HIM.
AND OH, SHE'D KEPT HIM *DOWN* ALL THAT TIME. *RESTRAINT*-- THAT'S *HER* GIFT.
SHE *OUTSHONE* HIM. KEPT HIM *STUPID*. TORE DOWN HIS *INSTINCTS* AND HIS *PRIDE*. MADE HIM A *SLAVE*. *PROGRAMMED HIM* SO HARD THAT EVEN WHEN HE BROKE *FREE*, EVEN *THEN*--
NRRRAAAAAAAAAAAAA--
HE COULDN'T *FINISH* HER.

YOU KNOW WHAT *I* THINK, DIARY? THE *CROSSED*. THEY'RE...
...OH, *PISS IT*, IT DOESN'T *MATTER* WHAT THEY ARE. IT NEVER *HAS*. IT'S WHAT THEY *DO*.
WHERE *WHEEERE!?*
WORSE-- IT'S THE *FACT* THAT THEY *DO*. THE FACT THAT "*THEY DO*" INSTEAD OF "*THEY THINK*". YOU SEE?

SHE BEAT THAT.
DIDN'T *NEED* TO BE *SMART*. DIDN'T NEED TO BE *SUPERCROSSED*.
JUST NEEDED TO BE ABLE TO SAY *NO*.
BUT THERE WERE ONLY *SO MANY TIMES* THEY'D *LISTEN*.
GO. FFFFFFFUCKOFFOFFOFFF HAAHHAHAHAHAH *BITCH*

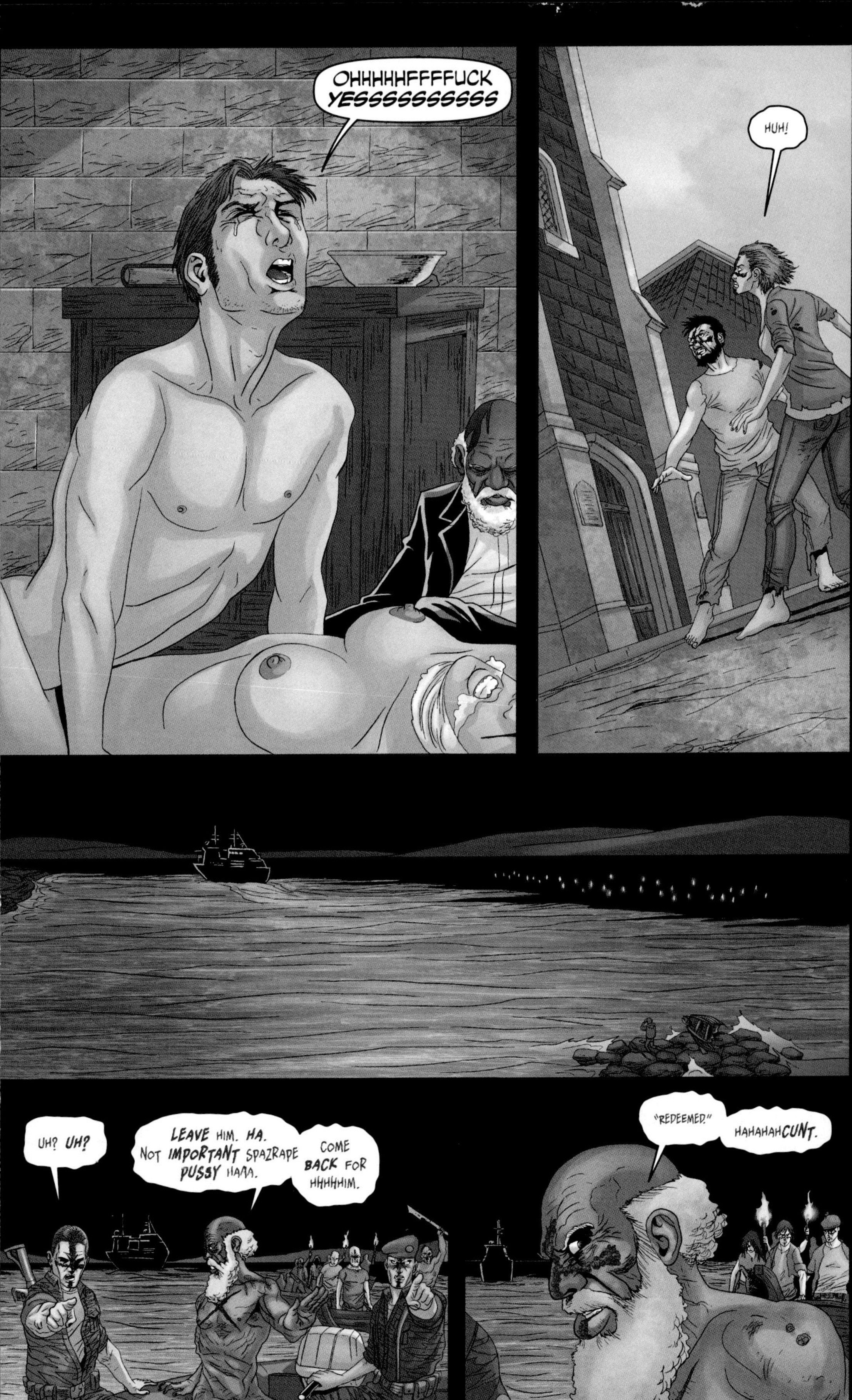
OHHHHHFFFFUCK YESSSSSSSSSS
HUH!
UH? UH?
LEAVE HIM. HA. NOT IMPORTANT SPAZRAPE PUSSY HAAA.
COME BACK FOR HHHHHIM.
"REDEEMED."
HAHAHAHCUNT.

AND THEN WE REALLY *HAD* RUN OUT OF WORDS.
JUST THE SOUNDS.

(SOUND OF... OF HER *GURGLING.*)
(SOUND OF A *DOOR* SMASHING SOMEWHERE DOWNSTAIRS.)

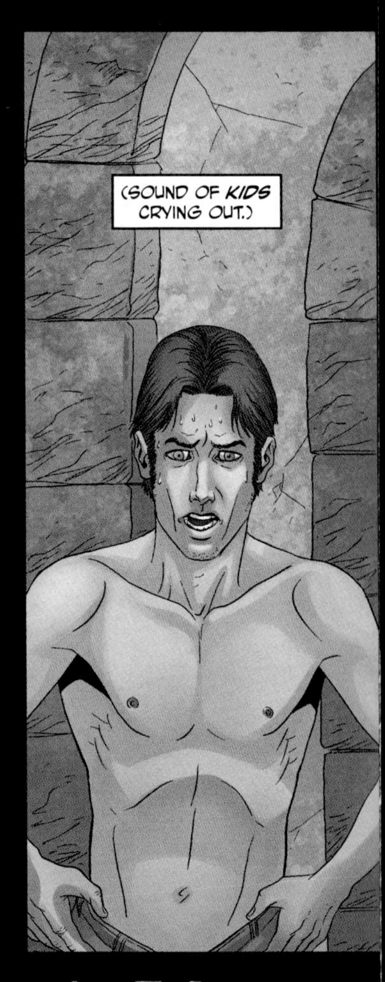
(SOUND OF *KIDS* CRYING OUT.)

AND I *AM*--
I TRULY, TRULY *AM*--
--SO, SO *SORRY.*

"IF I'M TO BE JUDGED BEFORE THE END OF ALL THINGS..."
"MYSTERIES MYSTERIES MYSTERIES."
"DAYDREAMERS NEVER LAST."
IT'S ALL THE SAME STORY. ALL MY DAFT LITTLE APHORISMS. OVER AND OVER.
IT'S THE STORY OF YOU, DIARY. ALWAYS HAS BEEN.
IT'S THE STORY OF DOOMED PEOPLE FINDING DOOMED WAYS TO DENY THE CHAOS.
TO TRAP IT IN PRETTY PATTERNS. TO THROW IT OUT OF FOCUS.
BUT THE CHAOS BUILDS ANYWAY, DOESN'T IT? IT CAN'T HELP IT. THAT GREAT LEVELLER.
THE CHAOS BUILDS UNTIL THE ILLUSION OF ORDER-- UNTIL THE TIDY HOLLYWOOD NARRATIVE - WON'T SUFFICE--
--AND THINGS BREAK DOWN.
AND WORDS FAIL.
AGAIN AND AGAIN.
FOREVER AND EVER.
IT IS THE STORY OF THE WORLD RECLAIMING ITS BALANCE.
THE STORY OF CRITICAL MASS.

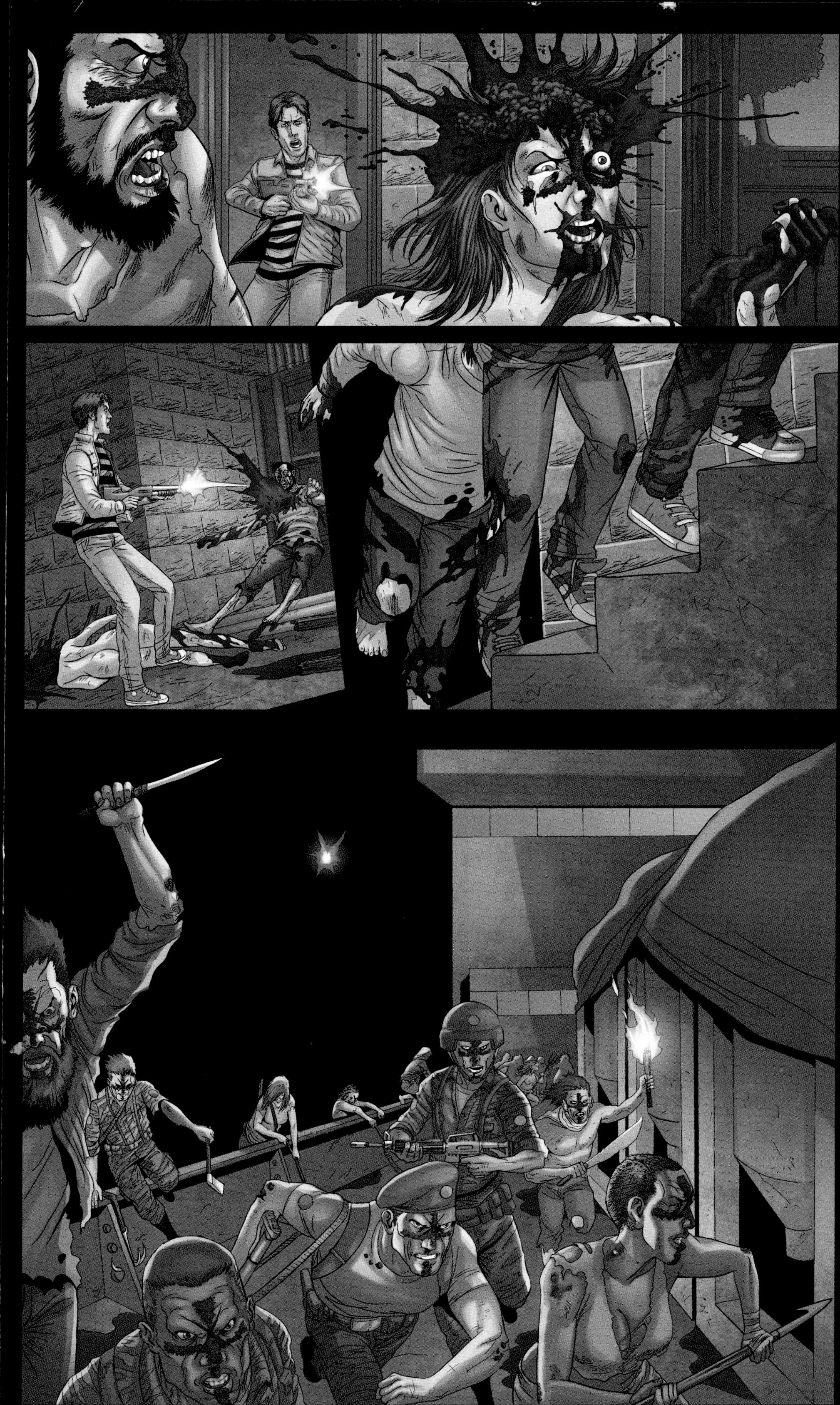

PHYLLIS.
MOIRA.
JAKE.
DANIEL.
...
WHERE ARE THE OTHER THR--

SOMEONE LAUGHED, DIARY. I REMEMBER THINKING IT SOUNDED LIKE A BIRD.
A DOOR SLAMMED. A TRAPDOOR-- HIGH ABOVE.

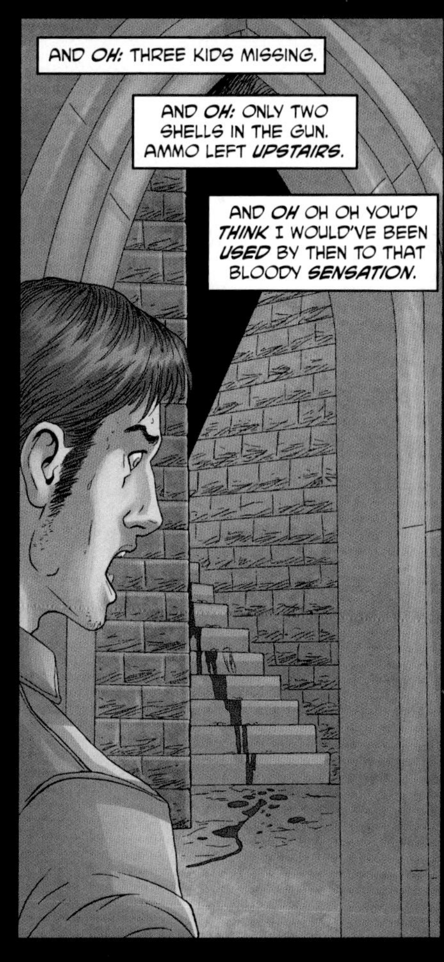

AND OH: THREE KIDS MISSING.
AND OH: ONLY TWO SHELLS IN THE GUN. AMMO LEFT UPSTAIRS.
AND OH OH OH YOU'D THINK I WOULD'VE BEEN USED BY THEN TO THAT BLOODY SENSATION.

THAT PLUNGE. THAT LURCH IN YOUR GUTS.
THAT OLD, OLD SINKING FEELING.

THE BOUNDARIES ALWAYS CRUMBLE. THE GREAT LEVELLER ALWAYS BUBBLES FREE, AND WHETHER QUIET OR LOUD IT'LL ALWAYS BEAT YOU.

I'M AN IDIOT FOR PRETENDING OTHERWISE. FOR TRYING TO BOX IT UP IN WORDS. FOR POINTING YOU INTO THE CHAOS, DIARY, LIKE NIGHT-VISION SPECS, TO MAKE SENSE OF THE SENSELESS.

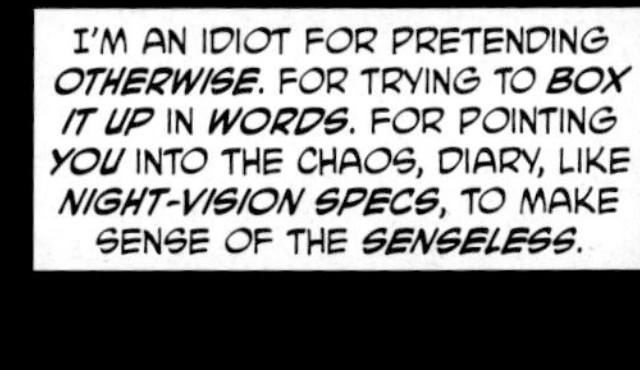

YOU CAN'T. IT'LL BEAT YOU AND BEAT YOU AND YOU CAN'T WIN AGAINST THE WORLD--

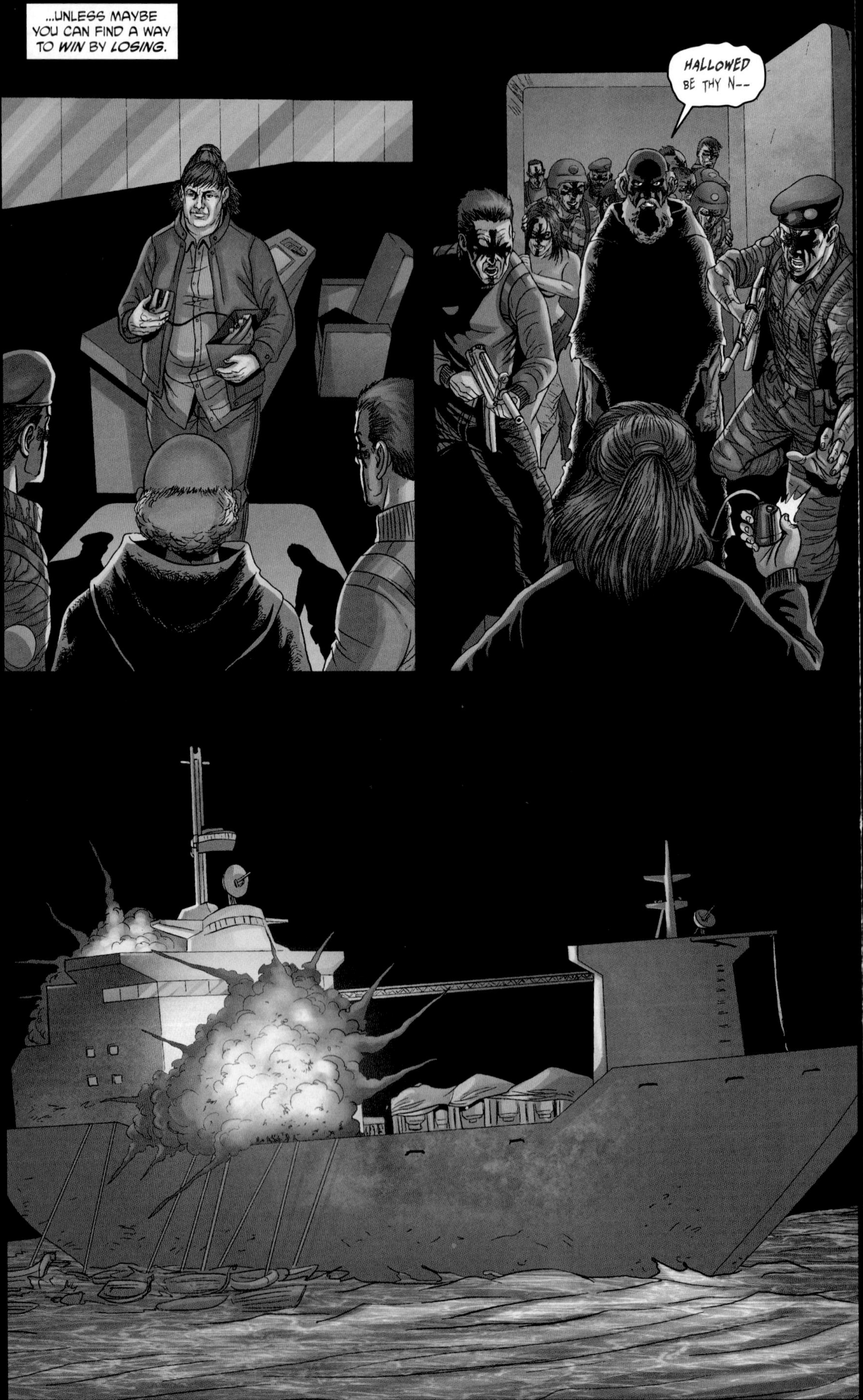

...UNLESS MAYBE YOU CAN FIND A WAY TO ***WIN*** BY ***LOSING***.

HALLOWED BE THY N--

OIL ON THE DECKS.
CLEVER.
CLEVER OLD RAB.
THEY BARELY NEEDED THE REFINERY AFTER ALL, DID THEY?
JUST ENOUGH DIESEL TO GET THE SHIP MOVING. SOMETHING FOR THE TERRIERS TO CHASE. JUST ENOUGH TO OPEN A MOUTH FOR THE CHAOS.
AND LEAVE IT TO EAT ITSELF.

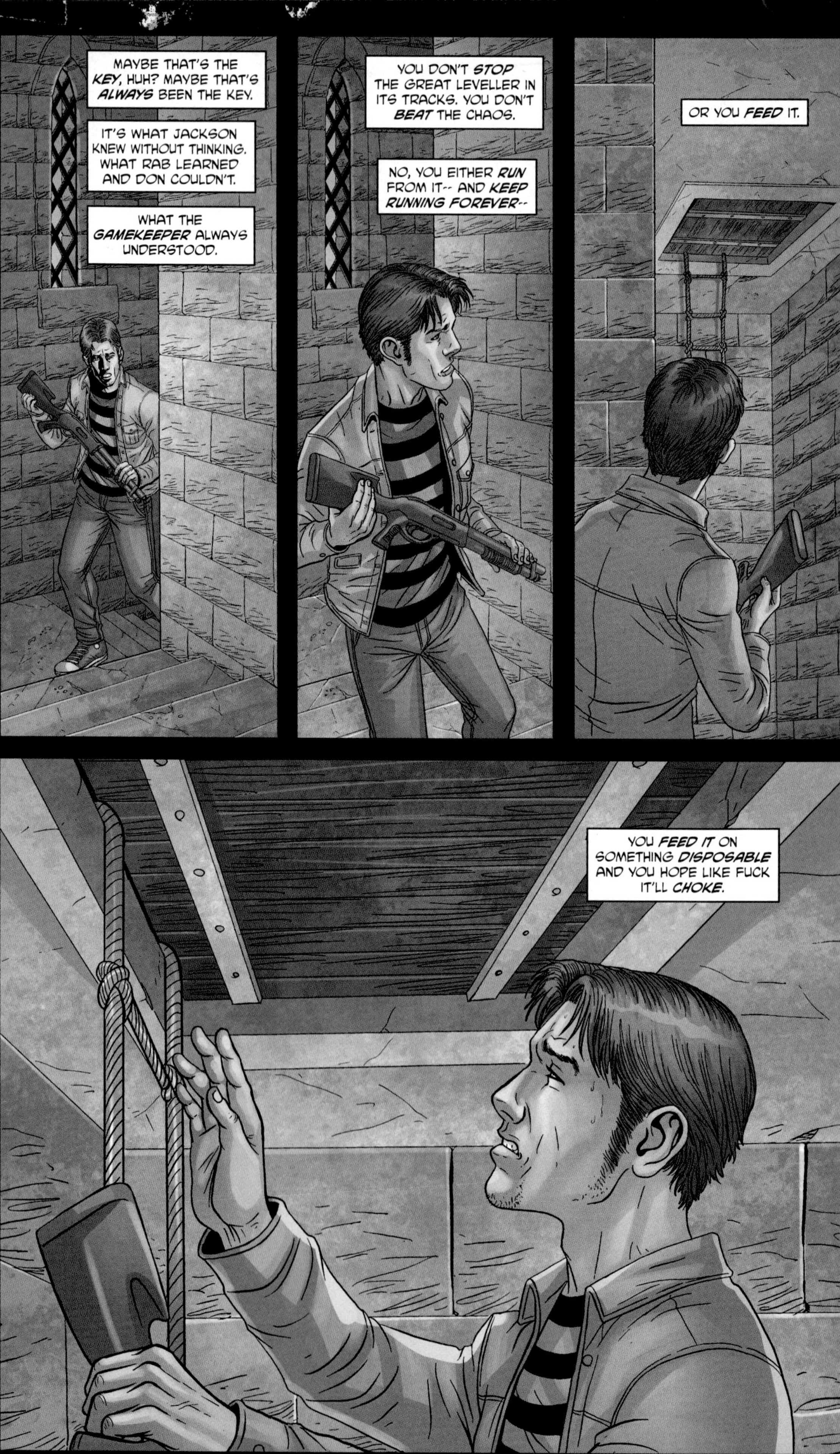
MAYBE THAT'S THE KEY, HUH? MAYBE THAT'S ALWAYS BEEN THE KEY.
IT'S WHAT JACKSON KNEW WITHOUT THINKING. WHAT RAB LEARNED AND DON COULDN'T.
WHAT THE GAMEKEEPER ALWAYS UNDERSTOOD.
YOU DON'T STOP THE GREAT LEVELLER IN ITS TRACKS. YOU DON'T BEAT THE CHAOS.
NO, YOU EITHER RUN FROM IT-- AND KEEP RUNNING FOREVER--
OR YOU FEED IT.
YOU FEED IT ON SOMETHING DISPOSABLE AND YOU HOPE LIKE FUCK IT'LL CHOKE.

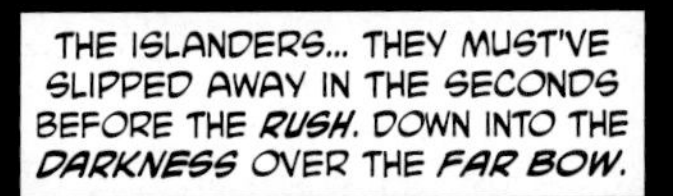
THE ISLANDERS... THEY MUST'VE SLIPPED AWAY IN THE SECONDS BEFORE THE *RUSH*. DOWN INTO THE *DARKNESS* OVER THE *FAR BOW*.

VOICES LOW.

HEADS *DOWN*.

OH, *RAB*. I WAS *WRONG*. YOU *DIDN'T* NEED ME, DID YOU? YOU DIDN'T NEED A *SNEAK*.
YOU *SLY*, WONDERFUL OLD BASTARD.

AND NOW YOU'RE *GONE*, CHIEF. YOU'VE *LEFT ME* AND SO'S THE *CHAOS*...
...SO I DON'T SUPPOSE IT *MATTERS* IF I *AWARD* MYSELF THE *TINY SATISFACTION* OF SUSPECTING THAT *MAYBE*... JUST *MAYBE*...?

...YOU LEARNED TO BE A *BASTARD* FROM THE *BEST*.

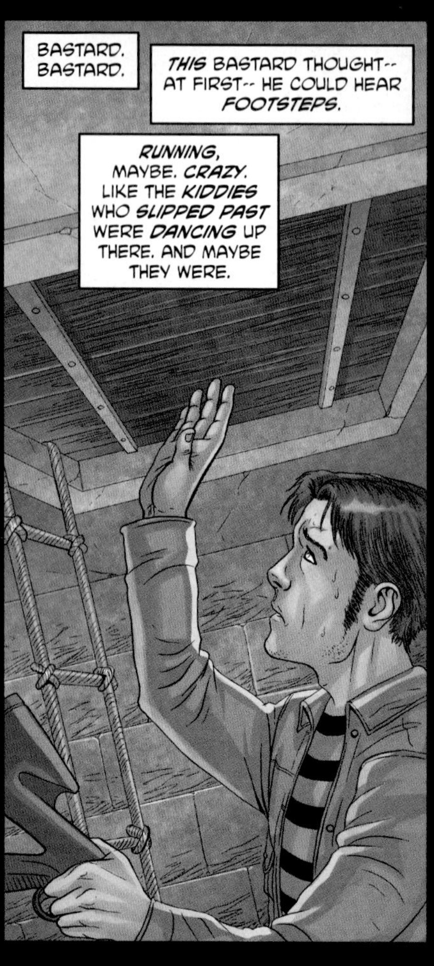
BASTARD.
BASTARD.
THIS BASTARD THOUGHT-- AT FIRST-- HE COULD HEAR FOOTSTEPS.
RUNNING, MAYBE. CRAZY. LIKE THE KIDDIES WHO SLIPPED PAST WERE DANCING UP THERE. AND MAYBE THEY WERE.

BUT THAT'S NOT WHAT I COULD HEAR, DIARY. I KNOW THAT NOW.
WHAT I COULD HEAR WAS ELBOWS AND KNEES. HER HEAD. HER ANKLES. CLATTERING AND THRASHING AT THE FLOOR.
FITTING AGAIN.

THE CHAOS: EATING ITSELF WHOLE.

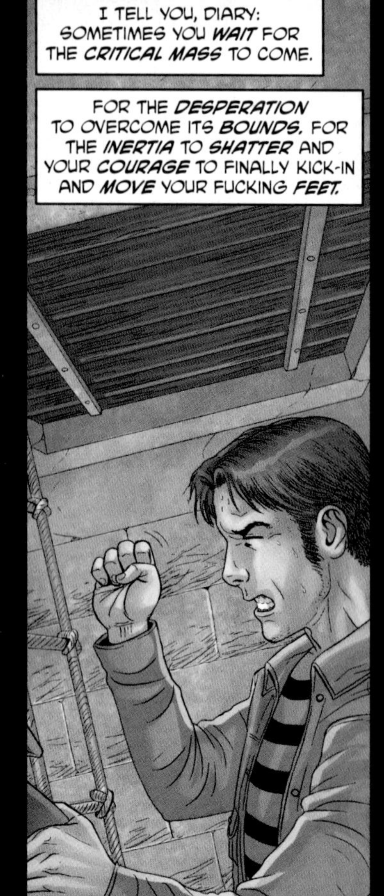
I TELL YOU, DIARY: SOMETIMES YOU WAIT FOR THE CRITICAL MASS TO COME.
FOR THE DESPERATION TO OVERCOME ITS BOUNDS. FOR THE INERTIA TO SHATTER AND YOUR COURAGE TO FINALLY KICK-IN AND MOVE YOUR FUCKING FEET.

SOMETIMES YOU WAIT FOR THE CRITICAL MASS--
AND IT JUST.

WON'T.
COME.
("IF I'M TO BE JUDGED BEFORE THE END OF ALL THINGS.")

DIARY.

HHH
CLIMB UP HELP HER HELP HER
I NEVER CLAIMED TO BE ANYTHING BUT A WEASEL AND A COWARD.

("IF I'M TO BE JUDGED BEFORE THE END OF ALL THINGS, I'D LIKE TO HAVE SOMETHING TO BE PROUD OF.")
I NEVER EXPECTED A PART TO PLAY. A MAJOR ROLE IN THE DRAMA.

MOVE MOVE MOVE
HAVE I BEEN PROACTIVE? UFF. DEBATABLE.

I'VE INSINUATED. I'VE NUDGED WHEN I SHOULD'VE GUIDED.
I'VE MANIPULATED INSTEAD OF MAKING DECISIONS.

PLEASE
PLEASE HELP HER
I HAVE WASTED MY STORY IN THE ACT OF WAITING.

BUT BECAUSE SHE IS BETTER THAN ME.
AND KIND. AND MERCIFUL.

HHHH
IN SPITE OF THE CHAOS. IN SPITE OF THE WOUNDS I'VE DEALT HER.
IN SPITE OF ALL THE EFFORT IT MUST HAVE COST HER TO COME.

SHE, DIARY...
(BLESS HER. BLESS HER HEART)

--SHE DOES NOT KEEP ME WAITING FOR LONG.

I-IS THERE... I MEAN.
ARE WE IN ANY *RUSH?*

...
...
No...
"...No RUSH."
THEN.
THEN H-HERE. IF. IF YOU *WANT*.
IT'S... IT'S ABOUT ME.
"IT'S ABOUT *US*."

SHE READS SLOWLY.
I WRITE THE LAST FEW WORDS-- FUCK, THESE WORDS, THESE FEW-- WHILE SHE GOES.
COWARD.
AT THE END OF EACH PAGE SHE TURNS TO LOOK ME IN THE EYE. SHE TEARS IT FROM THE SHEAF.
...AND SACRIFICES IT TO THE WIND.
WHAT I'M THINKING IS: "IF I'M TO BE JUDGED BEFORE THE END OF ALL THINGS, I'D LIKE TO HAVE SOMETHING TO BE PROUD OF."
SHE TOLD ME THAT, ONCE. IT FEELS IMPORTANT, HERE. A PURGING. A BENEDICTION. A GIFT OF VALIDATION.
IT FEELS MYTHIC, AND I WISH I WASN'T TOO SHIT A WRITER TO EXPLAIN WHY.
BUT I AM.
I'M SHIT AND I'M SITTING HERE AT THE FINISH AND DIARY I'M SPAFFING TOO MANY WORDS AND OH, OH GOD, I SO WANT A NEAT ENDING.
I SO WANT TO STOP IGNORING THE MYSTERIES AND START SOLVING THEM.
COWARD.

SO LET'S BE SYSTEMATIC ABOUT THIS.

SHE HAS AN "X" INSTEAD OF A PLUS. SHE THINKS AND CONTROLS AND RESTRAINS LIKE NONE OF THE REST.
SUPERCROSSED? SPECIAL STRAIN? SPARED BY GOD?
MUTANT SCI-FI WANKY ABERRATION CAUSED BY EPILEPTIC SEIZURE WHILE BEING REPEATEDLY MAULED BY THREE INFECTIOUS RUGRATS?

(WHILE. NOBODY. HELPED.)
FUCK OFF.

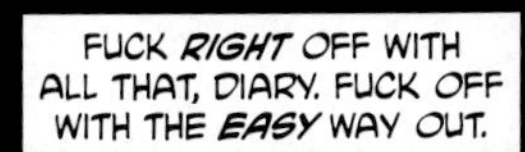
FUCK RIGHT OFF WITH ALL THAT, DIARY. FUCK OFF WITH THE EASY WAY OUT.

I THINK:

I THINK THE RASH GREW THE WAY IT DID BECAUSE THE GAMEKEEPER GAVE IT A SCAR TO SETTLE IN. I THINK SHE THINKS THE WAY SHE DOES BECAUSE SHE'S HER. I THINK IT DOESN'T MATTER A SINGLE TIRED TOSS ANYWAY.

I THINK MY BRAIN'S JUST BRIGHT ENOUGH TO KNOW THESE AREN'T THE RIGHT FUCKING MYSTERIES... BUT TOO DENSE TO KNOW WHICH ONES ARE.

WHAT ARE THE CROSSED? WHY ARE THE CROSSED?
MORE STUPID QUESTIONS. QUESTIONS WE'VE ALWAYS BEEN ABLE TO ANSWER EVEN IF THERE AREN'T THE WORDS TO SAY HOW.

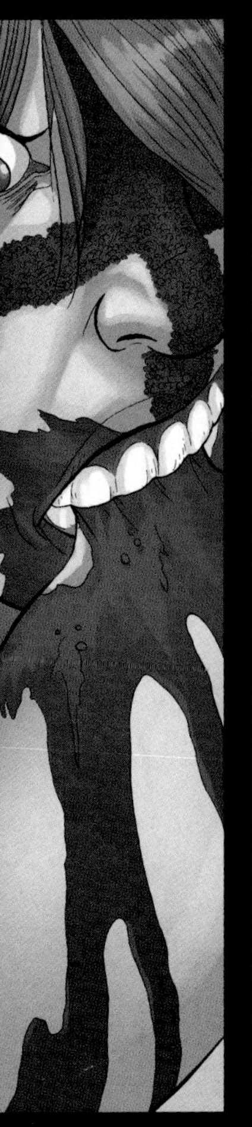

BUT WORDS ARE ALL I'VE GOT, AND AS THE WIND STEALS MY TIME I'M SPEWING THEM-- BEHOLD MY FINAL SALVO, DIARY! TO TRY AND AVOID... WHAT?
HA. OF COURSE. TO TRY AND AVOID AN UNSATISFYING CONCLUSION. THE STORYTELLER'S ULTIMATE SHAME.

THERE'S SOMETHING MYTHIC ABOUT THAT, TOO.

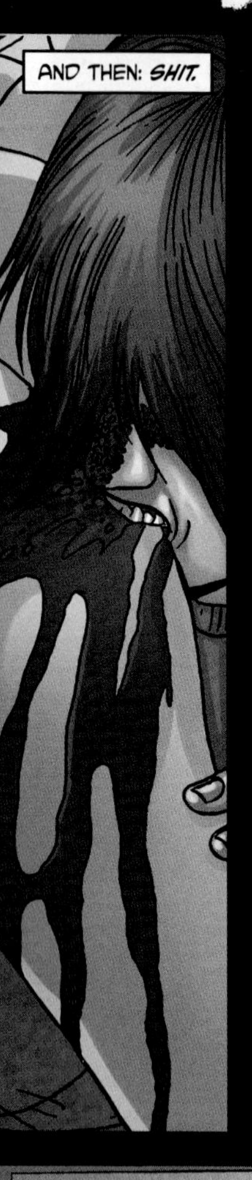
AND THEN: SHIT.

JUST AS I'M HOMING-IN ON A CLEVER SIGN-OFF, SOMETHING GROANS IN HER BOAT.
A TREMBLING HAND. THE BLOODIED DOME OF A HEAD: RECENTLY WHACKED.
AND I REALISE NOW WHERE SHE'S BEEN SINCE SHE DRIFTED OFF ALONE LAST NIGHT. WHAT PACKAGE SHE'S BEEN COLLECTING. WHAT GIFT SHE'S BROUGHT.

I DON'T ASK. SHE ANSWERS ANYWAY.
END.
END FOR HIM. ME. YOU.
HAD TO BE THE RIGHT END.
THAT'S WHY.
WHY EVERYTHING.

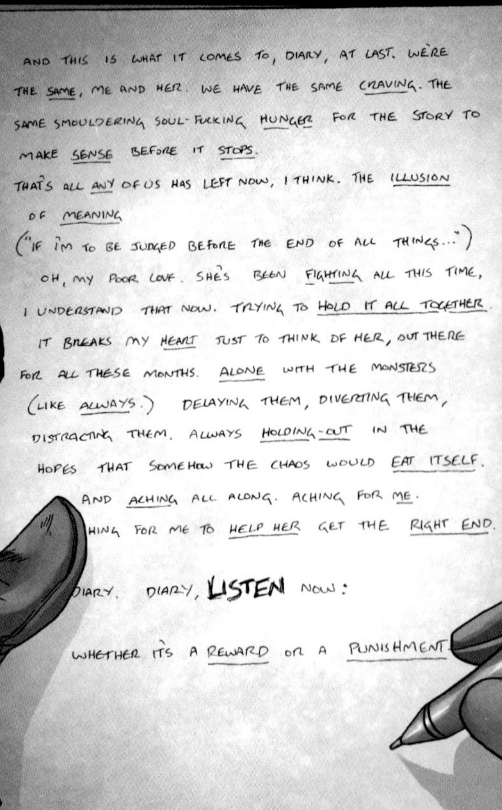
AND THIS IS WHAT IT COMES TO, DIARY, AT LAST. WE'RE THE SAME, ME AND HER. WE HAVE THE SAME CRAVING. THE SAME SMOULDERING SOUL-FUCKING HUNGER FOR THE STORY TO MAKE SENSE BEFORE IT STOPS.
THAT'S ALL ANY OF US HAS LEFT NOW, I THINK. THE ILLUSION OF MEANING
("IF I'M TO BE JUDGED BEFORE THE END OF ALL THINGS...")
OH, MY POOR LOVE. SHE'S BEEN FIGHTING ALL THIS TIME, I UNDERSTAND THAT NOW. TRYING TO HOLD IT ALL TOGETHER.
IT BREAKS MY HEART JUST TO THINK OF HER, OUT THERE FOR ALL THESE MONTHS. ALONE WITH THE MONSTERS (LIKE ALWAYS.) DELAYING THEM, DIVERTING THEM, DISTRACTING THEM. ALWAYS HOLDING-OUT IN THE HOPES THAT SOMEHOW THE CHAOS WOULD EAT ITSELF.
AND ACHING ALL ALONG. ACHING FOR ME.
HING FOR ME TO HELP HER GET THE RIGHT END.
IARY. DIARY, LISTEN NOW:
WHETHER IT'S A REWARD OR A PUNISHMENT

--JUSTICE DOESN'T GET TO BE RANDOM.
I CAN'T FINISH IT.
HE WON'T.
YOU MUST.
JUSTICE ISN'T JUSTICE UNLESS IT COMES FROM SOMEONE WHO KNOWS THE WHOLE STORY.

PUNISHMENT.
REWARD.

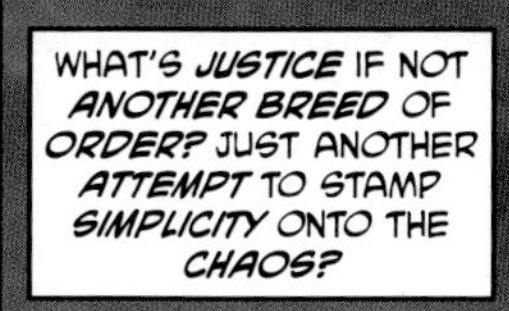
WHAT'S JUSTICE IF NOT ANOTHER BREED OF ORDER? JUST ANOTHER ATTEMPT TO STAMP SIMPLICITY ONTO THE CHAOS?

(HA. I DO BELIEVE I SMELL A LAST-MINUTE CONCLUSION FORMING AFTER ALL, DIARY, TO SPARE US THE INDIGNITY OF A FIZZLING FINALE.)

JUSTICE.
ORDER.
SIMPLICITY.

ALL THE ROUTINES AND REGULATIONS OF CAVA. ALL THE ATTEMPTS TO RECORD AND INTERPRET. ALL THE REPEATED-LINES. ALL THE TURNS OF PHRASE.
ALL JUST STORIES. STORIES TRYING TO INFLICT TIDINESS ON AN UNTIDY WORLD.
EVERY BREATH. EVERY PAGE. EVERY WORD.

ALL JUST ISLANDS. DOOMED ISLANDS.
BRIEFLY HOLDING OUT AGAINST THE DARK.

W-WHAT DO YOU THINK?
IS IT A GOOD STORY?

MM?
OH.
DIDN'T READ IT.

JUST COUNTED THE WORDS.

STOP CRYING.
I'M SORRY. I'M SORRY. I'M SO S--
STOP TALKING.

NO MORE WORDS.
BE THE JUDGE, MY LOVE. PUNISHMENTS AND REWARDS.
YOUR MESS. YOUR RESPONSIBILITY. YOUR DUTY.
GIVE.
US.
ALL.

"AN END."

THEY STILL *THERE?*

AYE. THEY'RE STILL *THERE*.
WHY? WHAT ARE THEY *DOING?*

WE-ELL, SHAKY'S... *AH*. LOOKS LIKE HE'S PULLIN' SOMETHIN' OOT AY TH'*BOAT*.
TELL US WHAT YOU CAN *SEE!*
RAB! BE MORE *SPECIFIC!*

I THINK IT'S... *HHHH*.
WELL IT LOOKS LIKE A MAN, IF YE MUST KNOW.

A BALDIE FELLER. HE'S... HE'S STRUGGLIN' A WEE BIT.
AND SHAKY'S GOT A... WHAT IS THAT?

WELL?
F-FLARE GUN, LASS.
IT WAS A FLARE GUN.
I-INTAE TH'BALDIE'S MOUTH.

HHH. TH'MAN'S HEID'S ON FIRE. HIS EYES'RE SMOKIN'.
HE CANNAE SCREAM.
AND THEY'RE...

THEY'RE PUSHING HIM BACK INTAE TH'BOAT. AND...
OCH, THEY'LL BE MAROONED...

SMOKE.
THEY'RE LETTING IT BURN.

A-AND NOW THEY'RE... THEY'RE...
AH.

WHAT?
I CAN HEAR SORT OF... *MOANING*. IS THAT *THEM?*
AYE.

LET ME *SEE*.
NO.
ARE THEY *KILLING* EACH OTHER?
NO.

N-NOW THEY'RE *SCREAMING*.
TOGETHER.
MM.

PLEASE LET ME SEE?
NO.
IT'S... IT'S ENOUGH T'BE *TOLD*.

REMEMBER THAT, *ALL* YOUSE.
ALWAYS REMEMBER THAT.

IS...IS THAT *LAUGHING* I CAN HEAR?
IT IS.
THEY'RE... THEY'RE HOULIN' *HANDS*. AN' NOW THEY'RE--

...
...

WELL.
WELL THEN.

THEY'VE GONE INTAE TH'*WATER*.

...
WH...WHAT DOES IT MEAN?
I DON'T KNOW, PET.
SOMETHIN'. MAYBE NOTHIN'.
SOMETIMES THE STORY'S ENOUGH, Y'KNOW?
SH... SHOULD WE GO HOME NOW?
I MEAN-- T-TO CAVA?
NO, LADDIE. I DON'T THINK WE SHOULD.
BUT IT'S... IT'S AN ISLAND.
IT'S SAFE.
AYE. MAYBE.
OR MAYBE NOT.
WHAT'S IMPORTANT T'REMEMBER, IS:

THERE ARE ALWAYS MORE ISLANDS.
THE END